The social construction of culture markets

Between incentives to creation and access to culture

Edited by:
Jordi López Sintas

The social construction of culture markets: Between incentives to creation and access to culture

Edited by: Jordi López Sintas
Universitat Autònoma de Barcelona
jordi.lopez@uab.es

1st edition © 2016 OmniaScience (Omnia Publisher SL)

www.omniascience.com

DOI: http://dx.doi.org/10.3926/oms.305

ISBN: 978-84-944673-1-8

Translated by: Ailish Maher (imradtranslating@gmail.com).

Cover design:: OmniaScience

Cover image: Water and waves © okalinichenko, Padlock design flat icon © Igarts, People walking in the street © tatoman – Fotolia.com

Acknowledgements

I wish to thank my colleagues in the Consumption, Markets and Culture research group at the Universitat Autònoma de Barcelona — including senior researchers, research students and graduate students — for all their efforts invested in making this book possible. I will not identify people by name as I would surely omit someone — but they know who they are and can be proud of their contributions to knowledge in this field.

I also would like to acknowledge material and other assistance from the Centre d'Estudis i de Recerca d'Humanitats (CERHUM) at the Universitat Autònoma de Barcelona, the European Union ERDF Programme, the Spanish Ministries of Education and Science and of Culture (whose names change with each change in government, thereby explaining slight nomenclature differences between the chapters), the Catalan Autonomous Government and the Agència de Gestió d'Ajuts Universitaris i de Recerca (AGAUR). Further details are provided in the Acknowledgements section of each chapter.

Thanks to our translator, Ailish Maher, who also copyedited the book as a whole. While she assumes full responsibility for any linguistic errors, I, as editor, and the authors assume full responsibility for content errors.

Finally, we wish to acknowledge permissions regarding parts of this book:

- Chapter 3 is an updated and shortened version of a chapter published in Spanish in Carlos Padrós-Reig and Jordi López-Sintas (Eds.), (2011), El Canon Digital a Debate. Revolución Teconológica y Consumo Cultural en un Nuevo Marco Jurídico-Económico (Chapter 5, pp. 169-246), reproduced with kind permission from Atelier Editorial (Barcelona).

- Chapter 4 is based on a presentation given at the 5th Vienna Music Business Research Days, 1-3 October 2014.

- Chapter 5, published in Consumption Markets and Culture, Volume 12, Issue 3, 2009, pp. 243-264, is reproduced with kind permission from Taylor Francis.

- Chapter 6 (a longer version of the article published in Poetics, Volume 46, October 2014, pp. 56-74) is reproduced with kind permission from Elsevier.

Minor changes were made, where and as necessary, to adapt these chapters to the style and purpose of this book.

Table of contents

PRESENTATION ... 7

Chapter 1

Access to cultural expressions and incentives to creativity: Arguments, evidence and implications
Jordi López-Sintas ... 11

Chapter 2

From the adulated author of antiquity to the powerful modern publisher
Jesús López-González ... 41

Chapter 3

The current Spanish intellectual property regime: The missing government syndrome?
Carlos Padrós-Reig ... 59

Chapter 4

The social construction of music markets: Copyright and technology in the digital age
Jordi López-Sintas, Ercilia García-Álvarez, Sheila Sánchez-Bergara ... 101

Chapter 5

A contextual theory of accessing music: Consumer behaviour and ethical arguments
Ercilia García-Álvarez, Jordi López-Sintas, Konstantina Zerva ... 123

Chapter 6

Music access patterns: A social interpretation based on consumption volume and linkage needs 161
Jordi López-Sintas, Àngel Cebollada-Frontera, Nela Filimon, Abaghan Ghahraman

Chapter 7

Law and economics of culture markets. Perspectives on incentives, selection, production and marketing
Jordi López-Sintas 209

Presentation

The seven chapters in this book describe our research into legal and economic aspects of markets for art and culture. We are particularly interested in problems associated with the selection of creations, incentives to creativity, (re) production of creations and consumer access to cultural expressions. The particular topics covered by the chapters of this book include questions of access to cultural expressions, the historical evolution of authors' rights, the current Spanish intellectual property regime, the social construction of music markets, a contextual theory regarding access to music and a social interpretation of music access patterns. Finally, the book concludes with a discussion of the particular issues raised in the previous chapters, namely, incentives, selection, production and marketing of cultural expressions.

Some chapters have previously been published in almost identical form in international journals (see Acknowledgements), whereas others have been written specifically for this book, which aims to offer a comprehensive vision of how cultural markets are socially constructed by the interplay between incentives to creation and rights of access to culture.

The chapters adopt a number of different perspectives: an economic perspective (Chapter 1); a sociolegal perspective (Chapters 2 and 4); a legal perspective (Chapter 3); an ethical perspective (Chapter 5); a sociological perspective (Chapter 6); and, finally, a blended economic-legal perspective (Chapter 7).

In Chapter 1, Jordi López-Sintas describes the theoretical arguments behind intellectual property legislation and reviews empirical evidence regarding its impact. He also analyses what would happen if the rights of creators and producers of cultural expressions were eliminated or reduced, assessing the implications of this new interpretation of the theoretical arguments underpinning intellectual property rights.

In Chapter 2, Jesús López-González considers the challenge posed by the digital technologies against the backdrop of how new technologies have historically led legislative developments and reforms and how authors' rights have evolved in the Anglo-Saxon and continental legal traditions.

In Chapter 3, Carlos Padrós-Reig analyses Spanish intellectual property legislation (and legislative reforms) and the functioning of collecting societies, mainly CEDRO and SGAE (responsible for music and books, respectively). Both these bodies operate as quasi-monopolies with little oversight by the government. Moreover, the lack of any proper mediation procedures effectively leaves parties with little option but to resort to the courts to settle disputes.

In Chapter 4, Jordi López-Sintas, Ercilia García-Álvarez and Sheila Sánchez-Bergara show how, with technological innovation acting as the initial driver of change, culture markets (in this case, for music) are socially constructed by legislative initiatives that respond to pressures from creators, producers, distributors and consumers. The transformation of local markets into national, then transnational and, finally, global markets has meant that the consumption of cultural expressions now transcends the limits imposed by locality, with legislation leading the way in converting cultural expressions into tradeable goods. The separation of the rights of creators and the rights of producers is suggested as a way to enhance incentives to creation while improving access to cultural expressions.

In Chapter 5, Ercilia García-Álvarez, Jordi López-Sintas and Konstantina Zerva analyse the moral arguments used by music consumers to justify their behaviour, with findings that suggest that the morality of accessing culture depends on the social, economic and cultural context in which an individual has been raised.

In Chapter 6, Jordi López-Sintas, Àngel Cebollada-Frontera, Nela Filimon and Abaghan Gharhaman analyse, using a theoretical model, the social dimension of access to music in terms of the substitution of purchased music by downloaded or copied music, with findings suggesting that access patterns, motivations and listening behaviours are structured by life stage and social position (as reflected by age and education).

Finally, Chapter 7, by Jordi López-Sintas, examines economic and legal perspectives on incentives, selection, production and marketing, highlighting the socially constructed nature of global culture markets and suggesting (as already done in Chapter 4) that the rights of creators should be distinguished from the rights of producers.

Jordi López-Sintas

Chapter 1

Access to cultural expressions and incentives to creativity: Arguments, evidence and implications

Jordi López-Sintas

Universitat Autònoma de Barcelona, Spain.
jordi.lopez@uab.es

Doi: http://dx.doi.org/10.3926/oms.298

How to cite this chapter

López-Sintas, J. (2015). Access to cultural expressions and incentives to creativity: Arguments, evidence and implications. In López-Sintas, J. (Ed.). *The social construction of culture markets: Between incentives to creation and access to culture.* Barcelona, Spain: OmniaScience. pp. 11-39.

Abstract

This chapter explores the role played by intellectual property legislation in the creation of cultural expressions (books, music, films, etc) and its influence on markets and access. We describe the theoretical arguments underpinning intellectual property laws, review the empirical evidence and reconsider arguments in light of the evidence. Finally, we propose a solution regarding the moral and pecuniary rights of creators and producers that would improve access to cultural creations while maintaining incentives to creativity. What we propose is to separate the pecuniary rights of creators from those of (re)producers and marketers, with the result that creators would increase their revenues, markets would become more competitive, access to cultural creations would be enhanced and the loss of social wellbeing resulting from temporary monopolies created and guaranteed by law would be limited. We also argue that transforming the moral rights of creators into rights of attribution would encourage the creation of derivative works that would enhance the popularity of original creators and possibly increase their revenues further.

Keywords

Intellectual property law, the economics of intellectual property, access to culture, incentives to cultural creation.

1. Introduction

The new digital technologies have altered the production costs of cultural expressions and how they are marketed and also offer alternative means for accessing cultural expressions. This situation has rekindled the debate regarding the protection of cultural expressions and the corresponding limitations on access. On the one hand, the growing availability of new technologies would suggest an undermining of the arguments in favour of protecting new cultural expressions (lower production costs); on the other hand, new technologies have facilitated access to, and sharing of, cultural expressions, thereby reducing producer and marketer control over traditional markets (lower marketing costs).

In this chapter we first describe the theoretical arguments behind intellectual property (IP) legislation — whose aim is to encourage innovation via what are referred to as a priori incentives — and then review empirical evidence regarding the impact of IP legislation on innovation. We show how incentives to the reproduction and marketing of cultural expressions change a posteriori when authors, (re)producers and marketers have legal rights but different interests.

We next reinterpret theoretical arguments underpinning IP legislation in order to determine what would happen if the IP rights of creators and producers of cultural expressions were eliminated or reduced. We demonstrate how inventions as created and marketed under the current IP protection system would likewise be created and marketed in a competitive system. This applies particularly to creations with sufficiently high demand for the author and producer to recoup incremental creation, production and marketing costs — in other words, creations that produce value for society and for creators. We argue that anything created in a monopolistic system would likewise be created in a competitive system — although naturally, profits for (re)producers and marketers would be lower in the competitive system.

Finally, we assess the implications of this new interpretation of the theoretical arguments underpinning IP protection and conclude with a summary of our main contributions.

2. Why Protect Creations and Inventions: The Theory

2.1. Incentives to Creation

The virtue of competitive markets is that they ensure efficient production and distribution. This means: (1) that once a material object has been produced and marketed, it will be consumed by those most willing to pay the established price; and (2) that the price will be equal to the opportunity cost of the marginal resources required to produce the good. Fulfilment of these two conditions ensures efficient resource allocation.

What happens when we apply the same reasoning to information, knowledge and cultural and digital goods? Preventing access to the good is only efficient if it means consumption by another consumer who values it more. For tangible goods, this goal is achieved by adjusting price so as to make the good available to the consumer willing to pay more. Intangible goods, however, such as information, knowledge, culture and digital content, can be consumed simultaneously by many people — say n people — and by even more people — in total $n+k$ people. However, preventing k additional people from consuming the good does not allocate resources from k (who value the good less) to n (who value the good more). If such goods were supplied in a perfectly competitive market, the price would tend to zero, all $n+k$ consumers would have access to the good and the outcome would be a socially efficient one.

Unfortunately, a zero price would not allow creators and innovators to cover their fixed costs; hence, in a market in which the only incentives were pecuniary, there would be no creators or inventors. The solution to this problem has been to convert creations and innovations into IP protected by legislation that allows a monopoly to exist for a certain period (Gallini & Scotchmer, 2002). However, a new problem arises, namely, the loss of wellbeing, which occurs when consumers with a reduced willingness to pay are denied access to the creation or invention due to its price being higher than the price they are willing to pay. Following the terminology used by Scotchmer (2004), in Figure 1, v (the area below the demand curve) represents the social value of a creation or invention for a specific period (one year, say). It is, thus, the sum of the values of all consumers, from the highest value (left, where the curve reaches its highest point on the horizontal axis) to the lowest value (right, where the curve intersects the horizontal axis at a price equal to zero).

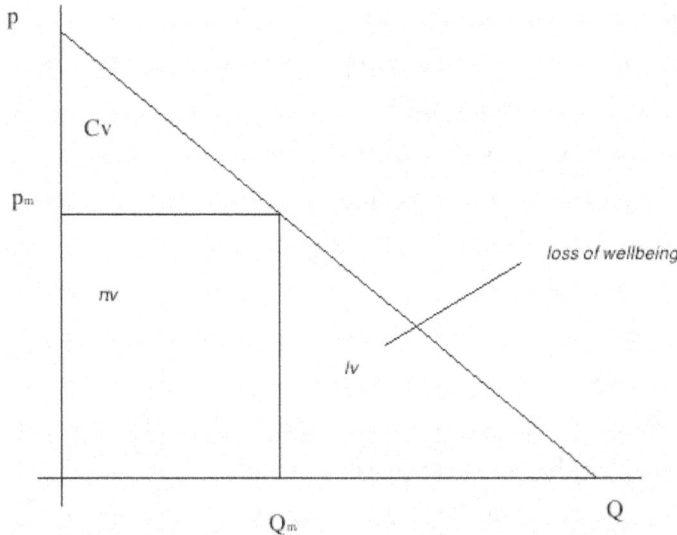

Figure 1. Value distribution between consumers and the creator/producer and the loss of wellbeing arising from restricted access to a creation

Figure 1 shows that we have to give up a part l of the social value of a creation or invention, which we call loss of wellbeing, lv. The rest of the area below the demand curve, $v-lv=(1-l)\,v$, is shared between the producer (πv) and consumers (Cv). The figure shows that the higher the monopoly price set by the creator, P_m, the greater the loss of wellbeing, reflected by an increase in size of the triangular area lv.

IP protection has the great virtue that the cost of an invention or creation is supported by consumers through the market price rather than by taxpayers through taxation, which means that the inherent risk is supported by creators and consumers, not by society. For simplicity sake, we will, like O'Donoghue,

Scotchmer and Thisse (1998), separate the exogenous idea creation process from the decision to invest in a creation.

2.2. Selecting Inventions

We denote an idea by the pair (v,c), where v is the social value of the idea for a period of time and c is the cost of turning that idea into an innovation, invention or cultural expression. Figure 2 depicts all the ideas that could be implemented as cultural expressions or innovations. If an idea has indefinite demand over time, its present discounted social value (present social value) will be $S=v/r$, where v is the social value of the innovation or invention for one period (held constant for simplicity sake) and where $1/r$ is the present value of a currency that remains constant for a very long period of time. Hence, v/r is the present value of v (see technical note 2.8.1 in Scotchmer, 2004). It would be socially desirable to implement all projects whose present social value is greater than their cost. The line $c=S=v/r$ divides projects according to whether cost is lower or higher than the present social value. Hence, socially desirable projects are represented by $c<S=v/r$ and socially undesirable projects are represented by $c>S=v/r$. The cost of a project on the left side of the dividing line — for instance, (v_1,c_1) — is higher than the present value of the associated profits; the reverse is true for projects on the right side of the line, $c<S$, which should be implemented as profitable for society.

Access to cultural expressions and incentives to creativity: Arguments, evidence and implications

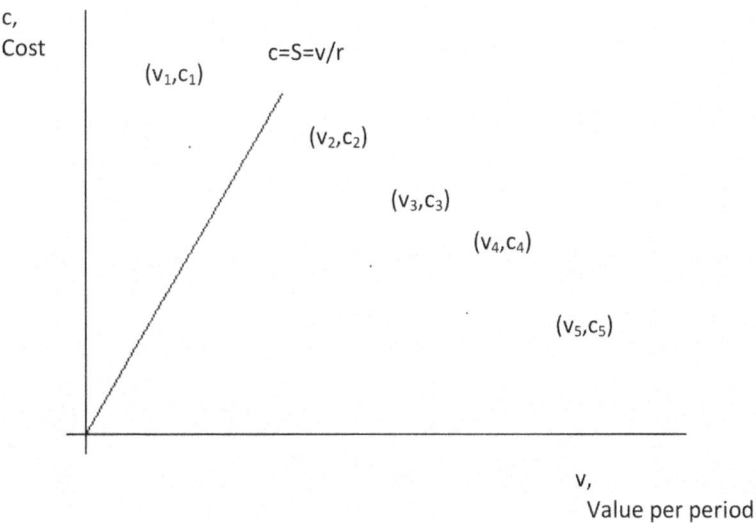

Figure 2. Selecting socially desirable projects

The current IP system grants private rights to innovators to encourage them to invest in socially desirable projects. Figure 3 shows the area under the demand curve, v, divided into the consumer surplus (Cv), the producer surplus (πv) and the loss in wellbeing (lv). The current IP system guarantees private producers a proportion of the total social value of the invention for a period of time T equal to $\pi vT < \pi v/r$, so as to theoretically cover fixed costs — as depicted in Figure 3, where $\pi vT > c$ (a simplification that does not alter the outcome of our argument). In other words, the IP rights holder can obtain a fraction π of the social profits per period v and can benefit from them over a period of time T. The producer and consumer surpluses and the loss in wellbeing (π, C and l, respectively) all depend on the monopoly price, p_m, and on demand at this price, Q_m. As we saw earlier, the higher the monopoly price, the greater the loss in wellbeing l, the lower the consumer surplus C and the higher the producer surplus, that is, the proportion π of the social profits per period yielded by the invention.

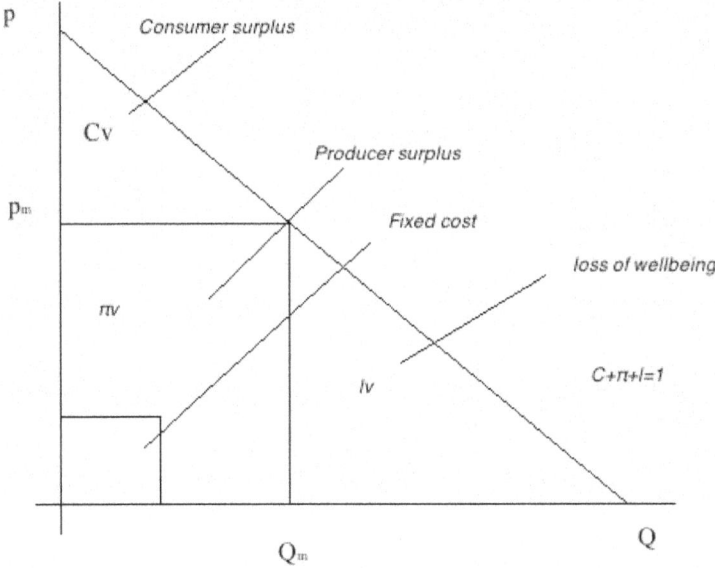

Figure 3. The producer surplus yielded by IP protection must be high enough to cover the fix costs of creation

2.3. Duration of IP Protection

Recall that the purpose of IP protection is to encourage the creation of socially profitable cultural and intellectual expressions — not to make them profitable over and above the profits that would be obtained in a perfectly competitive market, that is, zero profits once all production factors are covered at their opportunity cost. In Figure 4, the line $c=\pi v T$ divides ideas into two groups: (1) those whose development will be encouraged, that is, (v_3,c_3), (v_4,c_4) and (v_5,c_5); and (2) those whose development will not be encouraged, that is, (v_1,c_1) and (v_2,c_2). The fact that the monopolist can only appropriate a proportion π of the social value v of the invention during T periods means that not all socially desirable inventions will be profitable for the private sector.

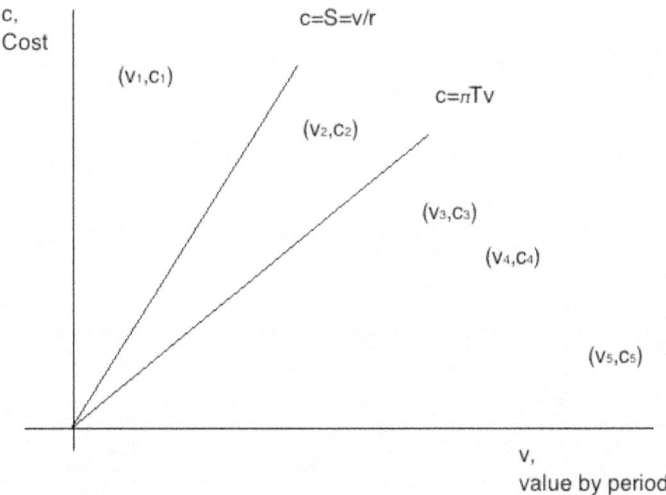

Figure 4. Inventions that would be financed given IP protection and a monopoly price

Thus, Figure 4 shows that project (v_1,c_1) will not be funded by the private sector because it is neither socially nor privately profitable. Neither is there an incentive to implement the socially desirable project (v_2,c_2), given that IP legislation would need to provide protection for a longer period than at present $(T_\delta > T)$ for this project to be privately profitable.

Figure 5 shows that if the IP system were to set the period of protection according to the fixed cost of developing and producing the invention, then T_a, T_b and T_δ, and even project (v_2,c_2), would be implemented by the private sector. The fundamental issue regarding the extension of protection periods is that we increase the loss of wellbeing per produced project, from lvT to $lv(T+\Delta T)$. Thus, an increase in the protection period, ΔT, would increase the number of viable projects but would also result in a greater loss in wellbeing. In short, there would be more inventions, but consumers who could not afford to pay the price set by the monopolistic producer would have to wait longer to access the invention or would have to access it in some other way.

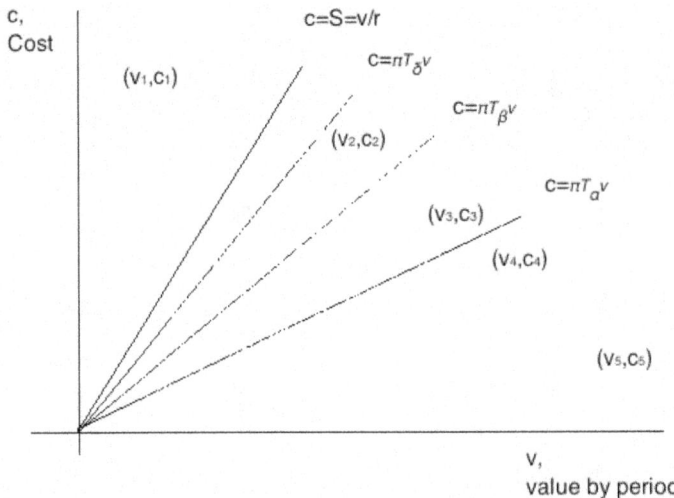

Figure 5. Inventions financed under different IP protection periods, T_α, T_β and T_δ

3. The Impact of IP Protection: The Evidence

IP legislation transforms an entire class of creative activities into privately owned intangible goods that can be bought, sold, resold, stolen and defended in the courts like any tangible good. This transformation, according to theoretical arguments, should increase the quantity of financed cultural productions. But has this in fact happened?

3.1. Creation of Culture Markets

Peterson, in a series of articles (1982, 1985, 1990), presented evidence of the impact of the US Copyright Act of 1909 in terms of restricting competition and converting traditional music markets into an industry. This new IP legislation protected the rights of owners of musical compositions for the first time.

Before the invention of the gramophone made recording possible, music publishers subsisted by reprinting sheet music for hit songs and appropriating the works of European composers who received no royalties for their works.

Musicians earned their living from public performances, initially in concerts and later on radio. The invention of the gramophone record and the possibility of making studio recordings theoretically expanded the market for all musicians. Every hit song produced by a record label, however, was followed up with as many versions as competing labels in the market. Music companies soon realized that they needed to own the musical creations in order to be able to retain exclusive rights over the (re)production and marketing of hits.

Songwriters, but especially publishers and record labels, pressurized politicians to include musical creations and their performances in new IP legislation that transformed musical creations into goods that could be bought, sold and developed by owners under the protection of the law. On holding the rights to musical productions protected by law, writers and publishers could, according to Peterson, invest in the promotion of new songs, interpretations and versions, since other publishers and record labels could not legally create their own versions. Thus, record labels began to insist on rights transfers from musicians and performers before they started to work on the master recording. Ownership of musical creations and performances meant that record labels enjoyed a monopoly not only in their investment in musical productions but also in current and future creations. Musical creations and performances thus became goods protected by IP legislation which could now be (re)produced and marketed with total liberty and with the guarantee of appropriating the corresponding revenues. The evidence indicates that the new IP protection of writers and publishers led to a higher level of commercial activity that, in turn, led to innovation in musical genres, including in folk ballads but most especially in ragtime and jazz.

Unlike the European legislation of the time, the new American law also obliged songwriters to be compensated for the use of their music in public places such as concert halls, dance halls and restaurants, although it did not provide any mechanism for collecting the corresponding royalties. In 1914 a group of writers and publishers founded the American Society of Composers, Authors and Publishers (ASCAP) as a private body that would collect revenues from public use of musical creations. Although not very successful initially, by 1930 it had become very effective in controlling market access for new musical creations, particularly because it managed to impose that only music registered with ASCAP could be reproduced in Broadway musicals, radio broadcasts and Hollywood movies. By 1950, ASCAP, controlled by eight record labels, effectively decided which songs would reach the ears of the public.

3.2. Impact on Innovation and Creativity

Peterson (1990), in his description of the rise of rock music, provides evidence that the US Copyright Act of 1909 transformed the market for musical creations and that ASCAP, representing a handful of record labels, restricted musical innovation by exercising a monopoly and controlling what musical creations would reach the market (see Peterson & Berger 1971, 1975).

The ASCAP record labels shared an aesthetic that favoured themes of abstract love, performed in a strictly orthodox way with strong melodies and muted jazz rhythms. Peterson (1985, 1990) cites *Tea for Two, Stardust* and *Always* as illustrative of this aesthetic. The market, thus controlled, kept innovation at a minimum and audiences only heard ethically 'decent' and aesthetically 'good' music — which is to say, the music sold by the record labels supporting ASCAP. According to Peterson, certain music genres, including African-American blues, jazz, rhythm and blues and (later) soul, were systematically excluded from the media, along with the up-and-coming Latin and country music genres. As a result, new genres were filtered out with the result that they never reach mainstream audiences.

This exercise of monopoly reached such heights in 1939 that a network of radio stations — in dispute with ASCAP about fees for broadcasting ASCAP-registered songs — formed a rival body called Broadcast Music Inc (BMI). BMI immediately signed up numerous publishers, record labels and composers excluded from ASCAP, many of them representing the less mainstream genres mentioned above. Since ASCAP was unable to reach agreement with the radio stations regarding broadcasting fees, from 1940 all

ASCAP-licensed songs were banned from radio stations. Songs broadcast by BMI and the genres they represented thus gained substantial exposure to audiences for the first time in musical history. Even after ASCAP and the radio stations reached agreement, the latter continued to favour songs protected by BMI. From around this point it became possible to make a living as a composer or publisher in these alternative genres, which eventually merged to form the basis for rock.

Going further back in time to the 18th century, Scherer (2004) provides further evidence of the impact of IP protection on the creation of cultural expressions: remuneration of Beethoven and Schumann works was very similar even though only Beethoven compositions enjoyed IP protection and IP protection led to Verdi reducing his efforts as a composer. Leaving aside these specific examples, Scherer (2004) calculated the number of composers in periods before (1700-1752) and after (1767-1849) the introduction of IP legislation in the UK, drawing comparisons with Germany, Italy and Austria where IP legislation remained unchanged. The number of composers per million population dropped in all four countries, but the decline was most marked in the UK after copyright legislation was introduced. This would suggest that protection had a dampening effect on innovation. However, data for France points to a positive impact of legislation on innovation, suggesting the existence of some uncontrolled variable that could explain the difference in IP impact in the UK compared to France.

Boldrin and Levine (2008, 2009) argue that there is, at best, only very weak evidence to suggest that strengthening legal IP protection enhances creativity. Quite simply, the evidence suggests that innovative effort grows in line with market size. According to Kanwar and Evanson (2003), larger and richer countries invest a higher proportion of their gross domestic product (GDP) — reflecting a country's wealth — in research and development (R&D) than smaller and poorer countries, so they not only invest more in absolute terms but also in relative terms. Boldrin and Levine (2009) reanalysed the data of Kanwar and Evanson (2003) in order to take into account market size. Given R&D levels in 31 countries in the period

1981-1990, they suggested that greater legal IP protection increased the GDP share of expenditure on R&D, but only from low R&D-to-GDP ratios; for higher ratios the correlation between legal IP protection and innovation disappeared.

3.3. Influence on Content

Although there may be some uncertainty regarding whether IP protection positively affects the number of intellectual creations, data from various studies would support the thesis that IP legislation influences the content of what is invented or created.

Consider, for example, the impact of the change to IP legislation in the USA in 1891. According to Griswold (1981), US legislation protected local but not foreign writers until 1891, which meant, in practice, that publishers discriminated against US writers in favour of British writers. For US publishers it was more profitable and less risky to publish an American edition of a successful British novel than to publish an American novel: no royalties had to be paid and the British novel had already demonstrated its success. US authors thus had to write about topics of particular interest to US readers if they were to have any chance of being published. US publishers even privately hired British authors to edit their UK-published works so these could be launched in the US market almost immediately after launch in the UK market, while avoiding the payment of royalties to the UK publishers.

The International Copyright Act of 1891 led to an increase in publications of American authors and, therefore, a redistribution of revenues in their favour. It also led to a shift in the novelistic themes of American writers, as they were no longer forced to write only on topics of interest to US readers. IP protection thus led to a redistribution in both revenues and content and the new legislation designed to protect foreign productions also acted to protect domestic productions.

Moser (2003) provides further evidence of the impact of IP protection in an analysis of catalogues of innovations exhibited at trade fairs in the 19th century. The advantage of using such catalogues was that it was possible to count innovations in countries without IP protection. Moser's study of around 20,000 innovations in different industrial sectors suggests several effects, as follows:

1. *The number of innovations.* Of all the countries participating in the Crystal Palace Exhibition of 1851, Switzerland, at that time with no legal IP protection system, was notable in being ranked second in the number of innovations per capita. Moreover, countries with no legal IP protection system received more medals for outstanding innovations than countries with IP protection (Moser, 2003: page 3).

2. *The kind of innovation.* Countries with no legal IP protection systems developed more innovations in the small machinery, control instrument and food processing areas. Moser found that one in four innovations at the Crystal Palace Exhibition was a new solution for the small machinery and control instrument sectors for countries with no legal IP protection, while the proportion was one in seven for countries with legal IP protection. The reverse occurred with heavy machinery inventions, especially for the manufacturing and agricultural sectors. Indeed, when the Netherlands abolished IP protection in 1869, innovation in the food processing sector grew from 11% to 37% (Moser 2003: page 6).

3. *Revenue transfers.* Switzerland's economically most important industries — chemicals and textiles — opposed the introduction of legal IP protection for foreign patents, as it would have restricted use in Switzerland of processes invented in countries with a legal IP protection system.

4. Summary of the Impact of Intellectual Monopolies

The evidence suggests that IP protection legislation has effects as follows: (1) it transforms cultural expressions into goods that can be bought, sold and resold, thus creating a market for cultural expressions and for creators; (2) it increases the profitability of protected cultural expressions in the marketplace;

(3) it encourages investment in projects with low development costs and high demand in markets with little or no legal IP protection (the case of book publishers in the US and the chemicals and textiles industries in Switzerland); (4) it redistributes revenues (a) between individuals in the same market, that is, from consumers to rights holders, and (b) between creators in markets with different levels of IP protection, but always in favour of producers or marketers (right holders) operating in markets with less or no IP protection; and, finally, (5) it influences creativity, but only when innovation levels are low, given that the correlation between IP protection and innovation disappears at high levels of innovation.

4.1. Incentives to Creativity Once a Monopoly Has Legally Been Established

The loss in wellbeing resulting from intellectual monopolies is twofold: (1) the loss in wellbeing may be high if the marginal cost of producing the cultural expression is low; and (2) the incentive to innovate is lower than in a competitive situation in which incremental costs are low (that is, there is less incentive to republish works). The loss of social wellbeing has already been demonstrated in the previous pages. The reduced incentive to innovate can be demonstrated with a reinterpretation of the Arrow (1962) model.

4.2. Incentives to Creativity, Production and Revenue Distribution

We assume that the author assigns the rights to produce and subsequently reproduce and market the original (master copy) to the publisher. When the IP legislation does not separate author rights from (re)producer and marketer rights, the author assigns her rights during T periods of time to the publisher. In this case the situation (the scenario at present) is one of a temporary monopoly in reproduction. However, if the law granted the creator a monopoly over time T that could not be assigned to the (re)producer and marketer, we would have a free-entry market with competition in the (re)production and marketing of cultural expressions, with the author retaining her monopoly over time T.

In the case of a (re)production and marketing monopoly, the publisher retains the corresponding rights and only the monopolistic publisher can republish the work or sell the corresponding rights. Thus, a (re)production and marketing monopoly can be understood as a market with barriers to entry (created by IP legislation). In other words, a temporary monopoly situation exists due to the legal protection granted to ownership of cultural expressions. However, the entry of new firms with innovations by other creators is not impeded. This situation can, therefore, be interpreted as a monopolistic competitive situation, if not, in fact, a monopoly (see Justman & Meherez, 1984). We would argue that the incentive to republish is less in a (re)production and marketing monopoly with legal barriers to entry than in a competitive market without legal barriers to entry.

4.2.1. The Competitive (Re)production and Marketing Market

Assuming that costs are constant, the unit cost will be c for the first edition and c' for new editions, with $c'<c$. The fixed cost of publication, which is expected to be recouped with the first edition, is included in c but not in c'. Let us assume that the cost c of the first edition also includes an author royalty r. The sale price for the first edition in a competitive market will therefore be equal to the opportunity cost of production, that is, $p_c=c$. Assume that demand at price c is $q_c(p_c)$. Since the incremental cost of reedition is less than the incremental cost of the first edition (that is, $c'<c$), to prevent the entry of competitors, the price of the reedition should tend to the incremental cost of the reedition (that is, $p_c'=c'$) and publisher profits should tend to zero. However, the creator's revenues will increase with the reedition, since if $q_c<q_{c'}$, then the market for period t will grow by $q_{c'}-q_c$ and the creator's revenues will grow by $\Delta I=rq_{c'}-rq_c=r(q_{c'}-q_c)$. In other words, in a competitive market for (re)production and marketing, the publisher has an incentive to reduce the price of reeditions, with the outcome that both the consumer surplus and creator revenues increase. Depoorter, Holland and Somerstein (2009) provide

evidence corroborating this analysis, namely, that copyright-expired works are reprinted more often than copyrighted works.

4.2.2. The Monopolistic (Re)production and Marketing Market

In the case of a (re)production and marketing monopoly we assume that both demand, $q(p)$, and the increase in total revenues from selling an additional unit, incremental revenue $R(q)$, decrease; hence, the number of copies offered in a monopolistic market before reedition, $q_m,(p_m)$, given by the equation $R(q_m)=c$, will always be less than demand at a price equal to the incremental cost.

Similarly, after the first edition, the publisher's offer in a temporary (re)production and marketing monopoly will be $q'_m(p_m)$. Let us assume that the monopoly prices corresponding to supply q_m and q'_m are p_m and p'_m, respectively. Let us also assume that B and B' are the profits of the monopolistic publisher before reedition $(B=(p_m-c)\ q_m)$ and after reedition $(B'=(p'_m-c')\ q'_m)$. In this scenario, what will be the incremental profits to the publisher and the incremental revenues to the creator? The monopolistic publisher will increase profits by $B'-B>0$. The margin per unit sold will increase and the total sales volume will also increase — with the exact quantity depending on the elasticity of demand, the elasticity of the incremental revenue and the new incremental cost. Profits will always be positive, however. As for the creator, the variation in revenues will be the difference between first edition revenues, $I_m=rq_m$, and second edition revenues, $I'_m=rq'_m$, that is, $I'_m-I_m=r\ (q'_m-q_m)$. In other words, both revenues and revenue variation after reedition will clearly be lower than in a competitive market for the (re)production and marketing of cultural expressions, given that q_c' and q_c will be higher.

4.2.3. Comparison

Incentives for the publisher in the monopolistic market are positive but there is a loss in social wellbeing (reduced access to cultural expressions) that does not occur for the publisher operating in a competitive market. As for the creator, incentives are greater in the case of the competitive market as revenues will be higher. Furthermore, if the publisher has scarce resources and, as would be expected, aims to maximize profits regardless of the cultural productions from which profits derive (that is, not maximize profits for each production of each creator), then the revenues corresponding to less popular authors would be even lower. This is because the reedition cost must take into account the publisher's opportunity cost and resources. The reedition cost for a less profitable creator compared to a more profitable creator should take into account the cost of foregoing reedition for the former. This scenario becomes more likely as the publisher accumulates rights — although financial resources are unlikely to grow at the same pace. Thus, in a monopoly situation, less profitable creators transfer part of their revenues to more profitable creators and the more profitable creators receive less revenue than they would in a free-entry (re)production and marketing market. In a competitive market, however, publishers would have an incentive to republish works; indeed, there would be no such thing as less profitable creators, as all creators would yield the same profits — virtually zero. So, differences would be reduced between more and less successful (more and less popular) creators in the publisher's portfolio, especially when we bear in mind that a monopoly implies economies of scale in (re)production and marketing and so provides an incentive to produce celebrities.

5. The Paradox of Access to Culture Versus Incentives to Creativity

As Liivak (2010) points out, achieving the seemingly difficult balance between access to culture and incentives to creativity — at the centre of most political discussions about IP — is nothing less than a paradox. Once conventional wisdom has internalized this balance between reduced access due to IP protection and increased access incentivized by profits, it is easy to see why an IP system based on free entry may seem untenable: we inevitably think that socially desirable projects will not be implemented if pecuniary incentives are reduced and we erroneously believe that a free-entry market amounts to reduced IP protection and reduced incentives to private producers. In a free-entry system compared to a temporary monopoly we think that some projects will simply not be profitable. We use the model described above to illustrate the reasoning of Liivak (2010).

In Figure 6, note how project (v_3, c_3) is close to the incentive frontier for (re)production by a private publisher. If we reduce monopoly duration T, this project would not be funded. But here is the error in the argument. A free-entry system is not the same as a monopoly with a reduced period of IP protection. A balanced free-entry system does not make cultural creation unprofitable, it merely affects the amount of profits. A free-entry system indeed reduces profitability — but only for projects where revenues exceed the incremental production cost. Thus, it is feasible for new competitors to enter highly profitable markets where market size is such as to admit entry. For inventions for which a monopoly overpays creators and producers, free entry will attract new competitors to the point where it becomes unprofitable for further competitors to enter. In the case of unprofitable projects, like (v_3, c_3) in Figure 6, no firm would enter the market during a temporary monopoly, as the structure of production (costs) and marketing (revenues) and of the market itself (competition) would allow for just one project.

Access to cultural expressions and incentives to creativity: Arguments, evidence and implications

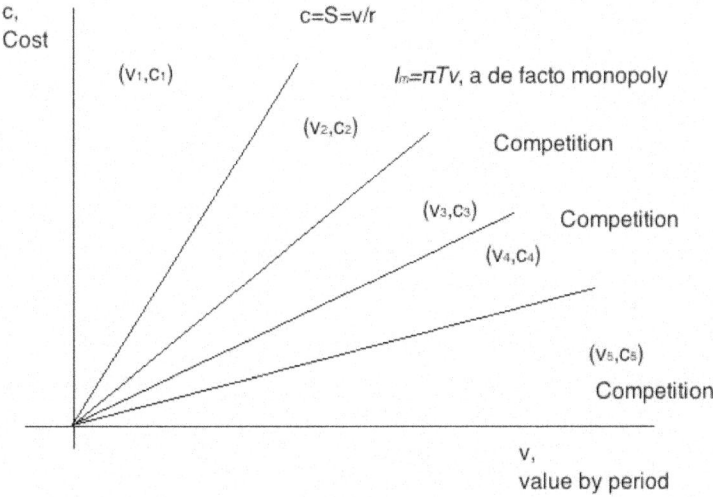

Figure 6. Incentives to creativity according to the duration of IP protection

In other words, for projects like (v_3, c_3), a free-entry system would, in fact, be rendered equivalent to a monopoly, as the market would have only one entrant. In contrast, for highly profitable projects with low creation, (re)production and marketing costs — like (v_5, c_5) in Figure 6 — a free-entry system would reduce profits but not creativity. Furthermore, in comparison to a monopolistic system, the loss of wellbeing would be less and the consumer surplus would be increased. That is, in regard to a priori incentives to innovation, the period of protection should be adjusted according to the incremental cost required to produce the creation. And in regard to a posteriori incentives to reproduce and market cultural expressions, IP legislation should establish separate periods of protection for creators and for (re)producers and marketers of cultural expressions. In other words, the protection period should reflect the production costs of inventions: the greater the incremental cost, the longer the period of legal protection of the rights of use of producers (Liivak, 2010) and the rights of attribution of creators (Depoorter et al., 2009). The impact of the new technologies is that they have greatly reduced the incremental costs of producing most cultural expressions on an industrial scale and they allow many cultural expressions to be reproduced digitally. All this would indicate that the duration of protection should be shortened (Lemley, 2009a; North, 2009). In sum, use rights (of producers) and ownership rights (of creators) need to be separated, first, to increase the revenues of creators and encourage innovation and, second, to enhance competition in (re)production and marketing and so increase access to cultural expressions (Vertinsky, 2009).

6. Implications

Research into access to cultural expressions demonstrates the following: (1) since many cultural expressions (those that can be produced digitally) share the properties of public goods, excluding consumers willing to pay less than the monopoly price does not improve resource allocation, as efficient allocation would respond to a price equal to the opportunity cost of production; (2) positive externalities of access to and consumption of cultural expressions favour the social integration of individuals sharing knowledge of these cultural expressions and may even strengthen self-identity (García-Álvarez, López-Sintas & Zerva, 2009a, 2009b); (3) excluded consumers who use alternative means to access cultural expressions would not necessarily be consumers if those alternative means were unavailable (even though producers mistakenly claim these consumers to represent lost sales); and (4) although copies or alternative means of access to cultural expressions are adequate substitutes in terms of sharing common properties of original products, they do not allow sharing of the symbolic properties that classify individuals in society.

Regarding incentives to creativity, in our arguments we have drawn a distinction between generation and production, (re)production and marketing. That is, we have treated innovations and creations as exogenous data and have focused on funding for their production, (re)production and marketing. The evidence presented above suggests that IP legislation that creates pecuniary rights attached to new creations has not been effective in encouraging innovation (Boldrin & Levine, 2008, 2009; Scherer, 2004). In fact, evidence from Depoorter et al. (2009) suggests that an increase in the number of creations (measured in terms of registered rights) only correlates with a population increase, whereas evidence from Kanwar and Evanson (2003) suggests that although IP protection does have a positive impact on innovation, this is only the case for low levels of innovation.

IP legislation has significantly influenced the kind of innovations produced and their profitability. Tougher IP protection laws have favoured capital-intensive innovations, with high fixed production costs for the first unit, over less capital-intensive innovations (Lemley, 2009b). In international markets, when innovations originate in states with different levels of IP protection, revenues are redistributed between creators and producers and both the consumer surplus and social wellbeing are increased.

Depoorter et al. (2009: page 1066) provide further evidence regarding the impact of IP protection. The increase in copyright duration in the period 1986-1998 in the USA affected the value of copyright-intensive corporations (Walt Disney, for instance) and obviously reduced wellbeing (regarding political aspects of IP protection, see North, 2009). Thus, IP legislation has transformed the cultural expressions market in such a way as to protect the interests of (re)producers and marketers, which, furthermore, constantly lobby to lengthen the period of legal protection of their temporary monopoly. Yet the evidence indicates that increasing the duration of protection does not increase the number of new creations, especially in large countries with high levels of innovation.

Complexity is greater when the cultural productions of different countries compete in the international market. Scotchmer (2004) suggests that producers from smaller countries with less IP protection benefit from greater IP protection in their home country and in the international market. However, conditions in the international market for cultural expressions belie her arguments; in the case of film and music, for instance, there is a cultural discount in exchange values outside of the original sociocultural context (García-Álvarez & López-Sintas, 2008). This asymmetric cultural discount is higher for smaller and lesser known cultures (such as Spain) and lower for larger and better known cultures (such as the USA). Therefore, as long as such asymmetries exist, it is strategically useful to maintain asymmetrical IP protection in markets.

So far we have considered the balance between incentives to creativity (dynamic efficiency), access to cultural expressions (static efficiency) and incentives to the reproduction of works (static efficiency). Given the evidence provided above, we ask how IP legislation could increase access to cultural expressions (that is, reduce loss of wellbeing and increase static efficiency in resource allocation) and simultaneously maintain incentives for the creation and production of new cultural expressions (that is, ensure dynamic efficiency in resource allocation), at the cost of lower profits for producers and greater revenues for creators.

If IP legislation did not grant exclusive (monopoly) rights for the (re)production of cultural expressions during a period of time T, the market price would reach equilibrium with the marginal cost of production. Access to cultural expressions would thus increase to the point of optimal resource allocation. In fact, as noted earlier, the evidence indicates that copyright-expired works are reprinted more often than copyrighted works. Furthermore, only a minority of books remain on sale after 20 years, for which reason, Burrows (1994) suggests that authorship rights be protected for 20 years and producer rights for only five years — but always taking into account the cost of producing the first unit (the master copy).

The temporary monopoly of symbolic expressions would therefore only be held by the first producer — who incurs the cost of producing the master copy of the cultural expression — and not by new entrants to the market who produce derivative works or reeditions. The distribution of profits between publishers would favour the first producer, who would obtain profits at least temporarily, while new entrants would obtain near-zero profits. Moreover, if the first producer wished to maintain the initial monopoly, they could always fix a price close to the marginal cost of the first edition (c in the model described above) and so discourage new entrants to the market. In fact, in reprints of a previously published book, Burrows (1994) suggests that original publishers have a cost advantage of 25% over competitors, that is, *(c–c')/c=0.25*. If the first producer was willing to allow other entrants to the market, they could always price the work at slightly higher than *c* for reeditions and so obtain a profit that was 25% greater. Since, at a slightly lower price than c, no competitor would reedit the work, the first producer would continue to enjoy good profits. At the country level, smaller and less innovative states would see their domestic markets grow in terms of both production and consumption and, hence, in terms of the revenues necessary for further domestic innovation.

Creators would obtain greater revenues due to the increase in market size. The fact that monopolistic demand would become competitive demand would likely increase creator revenues, irrespective of whether she participated in an international or domestic market. If, in addition, IP legislation restricted creators' moral rights to attribution rights (Depoorter et al., 2009), competition would lead to the creation of derivative works, which would, in turn, have a positive impact on the reputation and popularity of the original creators and likely bring them additional revenues from complementary activities. Derivative works (for instance, reprints) create publicity for the original work, although such works may be at a disadvantage in terms of costs and symbolic benefits for consumers.

Nonetheless, the problem remains of fair use/fair dealing regarding original works when the author does not share or authorize the derivative work. Moral rights as currently protected give creators the right to block derivative use of their works — despite the fact that all authors feed on previously created cultural expressions as part of their own cultural heritage. Indeed, their creations typically use known ingredients packaged in some new way. Limiting moral rights to attribution rights would protect the rights of original creators and would also safeguard them from any consequences arising from a derivative work. The right of attribution would indeed reduce the rights of creators to block use of their creations, but it would have the advantage of increasing access to cultural expressions and encouraging the creation of variations on the original work.

7. Conclusions

Although the theory suggests that access to cultural expressions has to be restricted to ensure incentives to creativity, recent reviews of the theory suggest that the temporary monopolies generated by IP legislation are neither useful (Liivak, 2010) nor the only way to enable producers to recoup the incremental costs incurred in innovating (Towse, 2001). Competition does not render such goods unprofitable, it merely reduces profits to near zero (although the resources used are remunerated). Meanwhile, access to cultural expressions is maximized, consumer surplus is increased and there is no loss of wellbeing resulting from the temporary monopoly

The laws governing IP, in fact, defend the interests of intermediaries who perform the tasks of (re)production and marketing (publishers, record labels, etc) more than the interests of creators. Legislation that eliminated the monopoly on (re)production and marketing of cultural expressions would increase access, eliminate the loss in wellbeing resulting from the monopoly and increase creator revenues.

Moreover, restricting authors' moral rights to rights of attribution would enhance their popularity (thanks to derivative works), foster the production of cultural expressions and facilitate market segmentation. Note that although cultural expressions share certain cultural properties, originals have certain symbolic properties that are not shared with copies and derivative works.

All this suggests that IP legislation needs to be reformed, yet it is clear that reform along the lines proposed here would encounter many obstacles, primarily from the disproportionately powerful (re)producers and marketers of cultural expressions. Indeed, much of the discussion about online access to cultural expressions is a consequence of the fact that producers and distributors of cultural expressions face losing control over the market.

Acknowledgments

This research has been possible thanks to funding from the Centre d'Estudis i de Recerca d'Humanitats (CERHUM) at the Universitat Autònoma de Barcelona, the European Union ERDF Programme and the Spanish Ministry of Education and Science (Research Project ECO2011-29558-C02-01-E) and the Catalan Autonomous Government/Agència de Gestió d'Ajuts Universitaris i de Recerca (AGAUR) (Grant 2014-SGR-502).

References

Arrow, K. (1962). Economic Welfare and the Allocation of Resources for Invention. In Nelson, R. (Ed.). *The Rate and Direction of Economic Activities: Economic and Social Factors.* Universities-National Bureau of Economic Research Conference Series. Princeton: Princeton University Press.

Boldrin, M., & Levine, D.K. (2008). *Against Intellectual Monopoly.* Cambridge: Cambridge University Press.

Boldrin, M., & Levine, D.K. (2009). Does Intellectual Monopoly Help Innovation? *Review of Law and Economics,* 5(3), 991-1024.
http://dx.doi.org/10.2202/1555-5879.1438

Burrows, P. (1994). Justice, Efficiency and Copyright in Cultural Goods. In Peacock, A., & Rizzo, I. (Eds.). *Cultural Economics and Cultural Policies.* Dordrecht/Boston/London: Kluwer Academic Publishers. 99-110.
http://dx.doi.org/10.1007/978-94-011-1140-9_8

Depoorter, B., Holland, A., & Somerstein, E. (2009). Copyright Abolition and Attribution. *Review of Law and Economics,* 5(3), 1063-1080.
http://dx.doi.org/10.2202/1555-5879.1439

Gallini, N., & Scotchmer, S. (2002), Intellectual Property: When is it the best incentive system? In Jaffe, A., Lerner, J., & Stern, S. *Policy and the Economy,* Vol. 2. National Bureau of Economic Research. 51-78.
http://ideas.repec.org/h/nbr/nberch/10785.html
http://dx.doi.org/10.1162/153134602753396976

García-Álvarez, E., & López-Sintas, J. (2008). La cinematografía ante el reto audiovisual: Políticas para mejorar la eficiencia productiva y reducir los fallos de comercialización. In López-Sintas, J., & Padrós, C. (Eds.). *Cinco ensayos de derecho y economía del cine.* Barcelona: Editorial Atelier. 11-42.

García-Álvarez, E., López-Sintas, J., & Zerva, K. (2009a). The Interaction between Culture and Social Structure: Interpreting the Micro-Social Processes Underlying Music Consumption. In Jaworski, J.A. (Ed.). *Advances in Sociology Research 7.* New York: Nova Publishers. 141-157.

García-Álvarez, E., López-Sintas, J., & Zerva, K. (2009b). A contextual theory of accessing music: Consumer behaviour and ethical arguments. *Consumption Markets and Culture,* 12(3), 243.
http://dx.doi.org/10.1080/10253860903063253

Griswold, W. (1981). American character of the American novel: an expansion of reflection theory in the sociology of literature. *American Journal of Sociology,* 86(4), 740-765.
http://dx.doi.org/10.1086/227315

Justman, M., & Mehrez, A. (1984). A closed loop analysis of competitive innovation. *Economics Letters,* 16(3-4), 339-344.
http://dx.doi.org/10.1016/0165-1765(84)90186-1

Kanwar, S., & Evenson, R. (2003). Does Intellectual Property Protection Spur Technological Change? *Oxford Economic Papers,* 55, 235-264.
http://dx.doi.org/10.1093/oep/55.2.235

Lemley, M.A. (2009a). A Cautious Defense of Intellectual Oligopoly with Fringe Competition. *Review of Law and Economics,* 5(3), 1025-1035.
http://dx.doi.org/10.2202/1555-5879.1436

Lemley, M.A. (2009b). Ex Ante Versus Ex Post Justifications for Intellectual Property. *UC Berkeley Public Law Research* Paper No. 144. University Chicago Law Review, 71, 129-149.
http://papers.ssrn.com/sol3/papers.cfm?abstract_id=494424

Liivak, O. (2010). Rethinking the Concept of Exclusion in Patent Law. *Cornell Law Faculty Publications.* Paper 599.
http://scholarship.law.cornell.edu/facpub/599

Moser, P. (2003). How do Patent Laws Influence Innovation? Evidence from Nineteenth-Century World Fairs. NBER Working Paper No. 9909. Published, in an abridged version, in *The American Economic Review,* 95, 1215-1236.

North, D.C. (2009). A Recommendation on How to Intelligently Approach Emerging Problems in Intellectual Property Systems. *Review of Law and Economics,* 5(3), 1131-1133.
http://dx.doi.org/10.2202/1555-5879.1435

O'Donoghue, T., Scotchmer, S., & Thisse, J.F. (1998). Patent Breadth, Patent Life and the Pace of Technological Progress. *Journal of Economics and Management Strategy,* 7(1), 1-32.
http://dx.doi.org/10.1162/105864098567317

Peterson, R.A. (1982). Five constraints on the production of culture: law, technology, market, organizational structure and occupational careers. *Journal of Popular Culture,* 16(2), 143-153.
http://dx.doi.org/10.1111/j.0022-3840.1982.1451443.x

Peterson, R.A. (1985). Six constraints on the production of literary works. *Poetics,* 14, 45-67.
http://dx.doi.org/10.1016/0304-422X(85)90004-X

Peterson, R.A. (1990). Why 1955? *Popular Music,* 9, 97-116.
http://dx.doi.org/10.1017/S0261143000003767

Peterson, R.A., & Berger, D. (1971). Entrepreneurship in organizations: evidence from the popular music industry. *Administrative Science,* 10(1), 97-107.
http://dx.doi.org/10.2307/2391293

Peterson, R.A., & Berger, D. (1975). Cycles in Symbolic Production: The case of popular music. *American Sociological Review,* 40, 158-173.
http://dx.doi.org/10.2307/2094343

Scherer, F.M. (2004). *Innovation and Growth: Schumpeterian Perspectives.* Cambridge: MIT Press.

Scotchmer, S. (2004). *Innovation and Incentives.* Cambridge: MIT Press.

Towse, R. (2001). *Creativity, Incentive and Reward: An Economic Analysis of Copyright and Culture in the Information Age.* UK and Northamptom: Edward Elgar Publishing.
http://dx.doi.org/10.4337/9781843767459

Vertinsky, L.S. (2009). Responding to the Challenges of "Against Intellectual Monopoly". *Review of Law and Economics,* 5(3), 1115-1129.
http://dx.doi.org/10.2202/1555-5879.1431

Chapter 2

From the adulated author of antiquity to the powerful modern publisher

Jesús López-González

Universitat Autònoma de Barcelona, Spain.
chuslopez@crearsa.com

Doi: http://dx.doi.org/10.3926/oms.299

How to cite this chapter

López-González, J. (2015). From the adulated author of antiquity to the powerful modern publisher. In López-Sintas, J. (Ed.). *The social construction of culture markets: Between incentives to creation and access to culture*. Barcelona, Spain: OmniaScience. pp. 41-57.

Abstract

In the modern world, intellectual property regulation needs to tackle the challenges posed by new technology, new devices and new ways of consuming culture. This is not the first time that intellectual property has faced a challenge of this nature: in early modern Europe, the invention of the printing press revolutionized how cultural creativity was understood and regulated. Intellectual property regulation is central to the relationship between creator and consumer. Below we summarize changes made to intellectual property regulation since the advent of the printing press, considering the attitudes held at different historical periods and how intellectual property is legally, socially and economically conceptualized in different countries.

Keywords

Intellectual property, copyright, technological change, cultural production, access to culture.

1. Adulation of the Author[1]

Copyright is an engine for social and cultural progress and for economic development. However, the concept of copyright is in a state of constant evolution and redefinition because it is a focus for many different interests. Rodríguez-Pardo (2003) observes that copyright is a concept that has changed and will continue to change over time, since it involves commercialization and creativity. There is no end to creativity, which will continue in our society and in societies to come as a response to the social and creative disquiet that exists in every period of history.

In Ancient Greek and Roman times, creators were viewed as deities and their works as divine creations. With the passage of time, this adulation continues unabated. Signs of the creations of these age-old cultures can still be found on the streets of Rome and Athens today, attracting the interest of both residents and tourists who come to pay homage to these ancient artefacts. In classical antiquity creators enjoyed a social status similar to that of celebrities today. They were recognized as the owners of their creations — a recognition that is today taken for granted and assumed without question. We have internalized the idea that artists own their work: it is part of our cultural imaginary and is rarely called into question. Nobody would expect Bruce Springsteen to give up his rights to the songs on his recent *High Hopes* album. Nobody would dare call into question the age-old status of authorship.

Creators, in return for pay, typically worked for wealthy individuals who, as patrons, funded the work of favoured artists. Without this patronage system, creators would not have been able to put food on the table or give life to the works that delighted their followers. Since they were subsidized, however, their creative processes were conditioned by the tastes of the patrons who commissioned works.

Recognition of the social value of a singular creative feat meant that artistic production acquired the aura of uniqueness. However, plagiarism — by secondary artists (the "pirates" of antiquity) who sought to achieve fame

---

[1] All translations of citations from untranslated works are by Ailish Maher.

by making copies of original works — threatened this uniqueness. To solve this problem, ownership of works was recognized so that nobody could modify a work without the permission of the owner.

Although no legislative measures were implemented to prevent plagiarism, a list of the circumstances in which plagiarism would constitute a legal offence was produced and punishments and penalties were applied, for the first time, to people who changed or manipulated an original work. From a personal and spiritual perspective, the work belonged to the author and usurping ownership, publishing without consent and plagiarism were illegal (Izzo, 2002). Falsifying authorship or making illegal copies of a work without permission were considered to be acts deserving of punishment (Baylos, as cited in Rogel, 1984).

The principles of what we now call moral authorship rights were thus established — even though these rights only extended to the social and not the legal sphere. Despite the punishments established for plagiarists, no legal protection as such existed, as it seems that arts and letters did not enjoy legal protection in Ancient Greece and Rome. Artists lived austerely and sought the protection of solvent individuals who could support them economically (Izzo, 2002). There was no recognizable legislative body to regulate these matters or the penalties imposed to redress any infringements.

The earliest agreements between authors and publishers regarding the use of a work were enacted as the first recognizable semblance of what would later become copyright. To ensure that their rights were protected, some authors transferred the power to sanction plagiarism to third parties. The Ancient Romans introduced a series of measures to underpin and define the author's status. Creators, the celebrities and stars of the period, were considered artists, no matter what discipline they worked in: "All were equally considered craftsmen, whether they created original works, or took inspiration from other works, or used forms and moulds for serial productions." (Calabi-Limentani, 1958). The author acquired a social status that was reflected in their remuneration (*pecunia*), their reputation and prestige (*gloria*) and the transcendence of their artistic works (*religio*).

The Ancient Romans, who considered art to be central to societal development, showed a keen interest in authors and artistic production: "There was a concern with prosecution in the event of a collision between two property rights: the right to the physical object including the creative act behind it, and the intellectual right to the creation." (Muñoz Mori, as cited in Padrós & López-Sintas, 2011). Formal recognition of the ownership of a work of art equated creation with other kinds of ownership; thus, ownership rights were extended to include ideas and the intellect as well as tangible goods. Both material and immaterial goods were thus deemed to be property in equal terms.

Authors, held in high regard in society for their honoured and privileged position, drew the adulation of admirers and of society at large and reaped the rewards in commissions from patrons. Publicity on their behalf sought to make them visible to the public. How publicity is achieved for creators may have grown in sophistication — but its objective remains the same: to persuade.

The principles of what we now refer to as author's rights were thus first recognized in Ancient Greek and Roman times. These principles are not substantially different today except for an exponentially larger global market. Although there was no specific intention to measure and define intellectual property in antiquity, there certainly was a concern to acknowledge the status of the author, which ultimately led to the development of ways to consolidate the author's position. Thus, steps were taken to ensure that citizens became aware of the owners of works and to foster values that honoured the author. Authors, thus rendered visible in society, became the central figure in the matter of rights and the justification for application of these rights. Very little has changed since then.

2. The Printing Press: A Paradigm Shift

The arrival of the printing press was a key historical moment in that it shifted the focus of rights from authors to the publishers who controlled the physical means of production: the printing press. Publishers therefore exercised direct control over what was published and so ultimately decided what texts would and would not be printed. Controlling the market, publishers eventually came to own and manage the economic rights over works.

By the Middle Ages the work of authors had acquired connotations of collectiveness: "the finished work was not the result of the activity of one person but of the contributions of an entire community — contributions which had no absolute material invisibility. We can therefore speak of a collective [contribution] in the modern sense of the term." (Vega-Vega, 1990). However, with the invention of the printing press this situation rapidly changed. Artistic production came to depend on machines that, relatively rapidly, could produce thousands of copies of a single manuscript. The spiritual aura and uniqueness of works produced individually or collectively was lost, to be replaced by reproduction and personalized use.

The invention of the printing press radically redefined roles and the balance of power regarding rights. Agents who managed contracts and the economic rights to works from the Classical Era — the main concern of these earlier publishers — emerged as key figures, gaining powers that are exercised right up to the present day. The fact that many copies of a manuscript could be made by a printing press at a lower cost than by hand changed society's perceptions of authors and their works and creativity and culture in general. The intellect lost its aura of spirituality[2] and creative significance.

Culture thus became yet another commodity that underwent different exploitation phases. Commodification and the ease of replication gave rise to a form of ownership governed by purely legal transactions controlled by a

---

2 To cite a Latin saying: *Ciencia donum Dei est, undi vendi non protest* (knowledge is a gift of God, therefore it cannot be sold).

small number of publishers. A new social model of financing and managing intellectual capital thus began to take shape (Sábada, 2008).

Content was managed in a feudal guild regime under the control of publishers. Securing ownership rights became the central objective in publishers' defence of the rights of authors. This right, known as a "privilege",[3] placed legal restrictions on printing and meant that copies could not be made unless one held the ownership rights. It was also the first measure that provided that a book could not be sold at a price other than that set by the publisher. The foundations were thus laid for a regulatory system that is broadly similar to that of today's globalized market.

The privilege system meant that the publisher had regulated monopolistic rights. The fact that right holders needed to grant their permission for anyone else to publish their work privatized rights in a work for the first time by law.

As Rodríguez-Pardo (2003) has pointed out, some of these principles continue to underpin the rights market today, namely, exclusive printing rights (monopoly), a time limit on copyright protection (temporary monopoly), legal measures aimed at preventing use by third parties (legal monopoly) and, finally, the right of printers to defend themselves in the event of a third party infraction (coercive powers).

The printing press thus brought about a dramatic change in how author's rights were perceived. Cultural production came to depend on those who held exclusive control over copies and content. The aura surrounding the author and creativity was dissipated, to be replaced by commodification in a market shaped by the laws of supply and demand.

Privilege provided the framework for early rights legislation by allowing exclusive use by means of temporary licences. This core principle has survived in the national legislation of many European countries to the present day. Indeed, the application of the privilege system to other territories is the origin of the different legal intellectual property instruments in existence today.

---

3   There were two forms of privilege. Simple privilege allowed the holder to print a specific work. General privilege allowed the holder to adapt or translate a manuscript before printing.

The first known record of legally granted privilege in relation to a specific work and a specific time period, according to Marandola (1998), was when Johannes of Speyer was awarded, in Italy in 1469, the exclusive printing rights for the letters of Cicero and Pliny for a period of five years. Italy was thus the first country to recognize the rights of a printer to exploit an author's work.

In Germany — Johannes of Speyer's own country of origin — privilege applied in each *Land*, but regional administrations worked together to overcome geographical boundaries, setting up agreements that would ensure that rights would be upheld throughout Germanic territory. Privileges were further consolidated in 1660 when penalties were established for illegal copying.

In England, the privilege system was established in 1529 (Patterson, 1968), when Henry VIII set a limit on imports of books from overseas and established a printing patent system ("King's privileges").[4] The Stationers' Charter was drawn up, granting privileges to the Stationers' Company and outlawing printing by anyone not registered with it. Eventually, when the interests of the Stationers' Company and the printing patent system came into conflict, the Star Chamber Decree of 1586 was passed, making it compulsory for all printers to register with the Stationers' Company. The Star Chamber Decree of 1637 further consolidated this monopoly by prohibiting the printing of any work that had not been previously registered with the Stationers' Company (Izzo, 2002).

This was the first time that a single company held all power over authorship rights on the basis of legal measures that secured the exclusivity of these same rights. The role of the Stationers' Company in England was similar to that of collecting societies later founded in other countries, such as the Società Italiana degli Autori ed Editori (SIAE) in Italy and the Sociedad General de Autores y Editores (SGAE) in Spain (founded in 1882 and 1889, respectively).

---

4 The patent system established two categories of rights: a general printing patent which was a licence referring to a group of works, and a printing patent which was a licence referring to a single book and lasting between six and ten years.

In Spain, the Catholic Kings, in enacting the Pragmática of 1502, established a system of privileges aimed at prohibiting the reprinting of works that were held under a printing monopoly (Baylos, as cited in Rogel, 1984). In 1558, 1569 and 1598 three further provisions were enacted to ensure that the right to set the price of a work was not violated. This control by publishers limited authors' rights to exploit and publish their own works.

Many other European countries developed privilege systems that protected the interests of publishers, with most conforming to the established pattern and implementing similar measures. This created a new balance of power underpinned by law: authors were demoted to a secondary role (as just another link in the production and distribution chain), while publishers consolidated their monopolistic position. Management societies or companies assumed a central role in a publishing business that privatized author's rights and consolidated them as yet another sector of the market economy.

Authors were no longer idolized as before, and, despite all the legal measures put in place to protect their rights, they wielded increasingly less influence regarding how their rights were managed. Publishers, meanwhile, consolidated their monopolistic position as gatekeepers, controlling what content was published.

Further legislative provisions would be founded on this initial disequilibrium that gave publishers exclusive powers regarding the selection and production of works and the rights over said works. The consequences of the legal and social construction of this market in rights remain with us today, with the main difference being that the market is far larger.

An economic perspective was thus incorporated into rights management. Ownership rights in purely economic terms became the main concern of companies that managed intellectual property — superseding the moral and economic interests of the author whenever economic interests failed to coincide. Access was key to control over works. Monopoly right holders controlled content, author access to the market and consumer access to productions. Book prices were set to maximize the profits of publishers and printers, not the revenues of authors.

The advent of the printing press is comparable to the more recent development of the Internet. In both cases, the question of access occupies centre-stage in rights management, with power deriving from control over access, whether by authors to the market or by consumers to the work. Since consumers are more interested in enjoyment than in material possession, the interests of both publishers and authors hinge on controlling access, which both parties do their utmost to ring-fence.

Thus, control over access has traditionally underpinned the development of rights legislation. Technological progress in the digital era, however, is affecting the traditional publisher's business model, as authors now have the means to directly access the market and consumers the means to access authors' works with no need for intermediation.

3. The Earliest Legislation: The Statute of Anne

The Statute of Anne, enacted in England in 1709, was the first law that established legislative and judicial control over copies of a work, thereby taking this power out of the hands of the Stationers' Company. The central objective of this legislation — which established a 14-year period that could be extended by a further 14 years if the author remained alive — was to eliminate existing monopolies and to recognize authors as owners both of their works and of the rights deriving from the same, including the right to authorize and freely select a publisher to reproduce their works.

The Statute of Anne thus revisited the issue of the rights of authors in relation to their own works. Izzo (2002) suggests that this represented the development of the new Anglo-Saxon concept of copyright, a term which first appeared in 1678 as two separate words, *copy* and *right*, referring to *right in copy* (ownership rights over the original copy) and *right to copy* (reproduction or copying rights).

During the term granted under the Statute of Anne, only authors and their chosen publishers could publish works; after the 14-year term had elapsed, authors were free to choose another publisher to represent their rights. The

Statute of Anne thus broke the publishers' monopoly, essentially rebalancing the distribution of power and restoring rights to authors by giving them a more central role. Publishers, demoted to a level beneath the author, were stripped of the powers they had acquired under the privilege system.

Despite the good intentions behind the legislation, however, publishers eventually came to manage the newly established copyright period. The Statute of Anne, intended to resolve conflict between publisher and author, in reality served to entrench the position of the publisher. The law did not explicitly strengthen the publishers' monopoly, nor was it intended to (quite the contrary), but, by recognizing copyright duration in law for the first time, it protected publishers' interests, as it enabled them to extend their control over authors' legitimate rights. The introduction of the notion of a copyright term — ostensibly to favour authors — would eventually become the grounds for defending the interests of publishers in subsequent legislation (for instance, in the US Copyright Term Extension Act, aka the Sonny Bono Act).

There was also a close-knit relationship between copyright and censorship, in that the publisher, as gatekeeper, could effectively decide what content was to be printed. Furthermore, postponement of the entry of works to the public domain limited consumer access while increasing the value of these works for publishers. In this way, publishers strengthened their control of the book market. A similar process unfolded in the music sector in the late 19th century.

Copyright legislation advanced markedly during the 18th century, particularly with the development of new laws defining copyright in terms of years. The English Copyright Act of 1814 set a term of 28 years or the natural life of the author if longer and the Copyright Amendment Act of 1842 increased the term to the life of the author plus seven years or to 42 years from the first publication of the work (whichever was longer). Extending the copyright term reinforced authors' rights and provided the perfect instrument for developing a market model. The objectives of the Statute of Anne were adequately met in that authors would receive payment for their work. However, although the reasons for extending copyright in time remain somewhat unclear, the outcome was that protection of the economic interests of the few was ensured, that is, of publishers.

These notions regarding copyright became the basis for a global market. Saunders (1992) points out how the spirit of this copyright legislation governing the British Isles was imported to the USA and inspired its own legislation. Between 1780 and 1787 certain legal concepts of the Magna Carta were introduced in the USA, with the US Constitution of 1787 favouring recognition of a collective right. According to Sábada (2008), the US adaptation of intellectual property rights in the 19th century was "an attempt to establish compensation for artistic creation while fostering collective progress — a conditional right". These collective rights were formulated in a way similar to the privilege system of the Germanic *Länder*. Thus, certain regional rights were guaranteed but were governed by general legislative principles. In 1790, the first Copyright Act of a federal nature, very much modelled on the Statute of Anne, unified copyright protection across the states and established the term as 14 years, plus the right to renewal for 14 further years if the author was still alive. Authors' rights were thus exercised from a dual perspective, that is, with consideration given to the particularities of each state and to a common national doctrine.

Copyright law today in the European Union (EU) has a similar, but not identical, territorial application. EU directives make recommendations aimed at harmonizing the national legislation of the member states, each of which establishes national principles governing intellectual property. However, whereas the USA shares a cultural imaginary, the EU has to grapple with several countries with their own historical, social and cultural realities.

In 1787 the US Congress began to regulate copyright, introducing some new developments in the field of copyright law. Its remit was "to promote the progress of science and the useful arts by securing for limited times to authors and inventors the exclusive right to their respective writings and discoveries" (Article I, Section 8, Clause 8 of the US Constitution, known as the Copyright

Clause[5]). Authorship and creativity both are thus fundamental concepts in US society, as reflected in US Constitutional and copyright legislation.

The Copyright Act of 1790 set out to define certain aspects of copyright, such as the owners of the rights to possession, access and the right to copy, protected uses and protected cultural expressions. It was thus the first law to recognize and clearly define core copyright concepts. Authors — citizens and residents of the USA — "of any map, chart, book or books already printed within these United States" and their "executors, administrators or assigns" who had "purchased or legally acquired the copyright of any (...) map, chart, book or books, in order to print, reprint, publish or vend the same" acquired the "sole right and liberty of printing, reprinting, publishing and vending such map, chart, book or books, for the term of 14 years." (Copyright Act of 1790[6]). In 1833 the rights to public performance and communication were included and in 1862 other cultural expressions, like musical creations, were included.

Thus, step by step, the concept of intellectual property was constructed, with copyright doctrine coming to define elements beyond the work itself and to include new uses and new cultural expressions. Access to works was no longer the only concern of publishers, and the powers awarded — over and above extension to the copyright term — had little to do with the work itself. Copyright gradually began to take the shape that we recognize today and was gradually extended to other creative endeavours. The proliferation of legislation continued up to the Copyright Act of 1976, which replaced and extended previous copyright legislation.

Although the US tradition in developing copyright legislation does not place the author centre-stage, it does encourage respect for the reputation and honour of authors. Nonetheless, the publisher holding most of the author's rights ends up benefiting most from this situation.

---

5   http://copyright.gov/title17/92preface.html.

6   http://copyright.gov/history/1790act.pdf.

4. The French Revolution and Continental Law

The other major school of thought (and legislation) in the intellectual property field is the continental system of law. In 1776 the *Memoire à consulter, pour les libraires & imprimeurs de Lyon, Rouen, Toulouse et Nimes, concernant les privileges de librairie, et continuations d'iceux* was published in France, defining where and when published works entered the public domain (Saunders, 1992). Under this system, in which authors were free to print and sell their own works, royal privilege ceased to exist in France (Muñoz Mori, as cited in Padrós & López-Sintas, 2011).

In 1791, the new French Assembly declared that creative productions would receive the same treatment as material property. Just as happened in the Anglo-Saxon tradition, creative property came to be commercialized, just like a house or any other type of property. The French Assembly also protected authors' rights to their works during their lifetime and for five years (later ten years) following their death. These measures aimed to protect immaterial works and authors' rights and also to recognize the cultural contributions of authors. In 1792 the National Assembly took another step forward in commodifying intellectual property by including music and other works as well as rights of reproduction and public communication.

The term *droit d'auteur*, used for the first time in public documents in 1838, reflected a dual principle of proprietary rights and moral rights. Whereas copyright defined the right to copy a work and extended the powers of the publisher, the aim of the French doctrine was not solely to control access to works but also to guarantee the moral rights of the author. This approach harked back to classical values that recognized the author's ownership of a work and respected its integrity. Although the *droit d'auteur* theoretically protects the two kinds of authors' rights in equal measure, it is the proprietary (economic) rights, which, under the pressures of the market economy, are most fiercely defended. In other words, recognition of an author's moral rights did not require foregoing the development of a market in intellectual property. The *droit d'auteur* system was, in fact, a system of privileges. Hence, given their similar origins in the privilege system, copyright and *droit d'auteur* are not so very different in conceptual terms.

5. Conclusions: Author Rights Today

Authors' rights have, over several centuries, been adapted to changing times, yet today we are experiencing a period of upheaval that can only be likened to the introduction of the printing press. Works, once material and unique, are now multimedia creations — a product of our time (Rodríguez-Pardo, 2003) — and the result of a technological revolution that is yielding innumerable novel means of expression and communication. The technological revolution has also led to new forms of commercial exploitation, most notably, digital practices that now affect how we understand and apply copyright. As in the past, we need to adapt to change, not shy away from it.

Common-law traditions are proving powerless in the face of the new technological challenges. In the desire to maintain the status quo of authors and publishers, the constitutional rights of citizens are being undermined. The Sinde Law and Lassalle Law in Spain, the Hadopi Law in France and SOPA in the USA have all proved controversial and have inspired protests by citizens calling into question the constitutionality of intellectual property legislation of this nature.

As for the continental legal tradition, although Izzo (2002) argues that this system does not award great importance to economic interests in a work, we would argue otherwise. The economic interests that inspired the system of privileges — which was the conceptual foundations for both copyright and the *droit d'auteur* — have come to contaminate and influence national intellectual property legislation in various parts of the world.

Today, economic interests hold sway in questions of authors' rights. The market responds accordingly and legislators are pressured to enact laws that are favourable to the interests of governments with interests aligned with those of commercial behemoths. The privatization of author's rights has been a reality since the advent of printing and, if the Internet follows the same trajectory as printing, it too will succumb to the same interests.

We need to reshape this exclusively economic perspective on the rights of authors so as to adapt it to the laws of free competition and to greater diversity in management terms. We can either choose to maintain the system that came into being in response to the printing press — provided it undergoes a profound review — or we can develop a new system, more suited to the modern age, that fosters healthy competition along the lines of Creative Commons licences.

Many challenges lie ahead, however, given that different national intellectual property legislative systems have apparently acceded to staunchly supporting the intellectual property model that gradually emerged after the development of the printing press and as yet incompletely adapted to the digital era.

Acknowledgments

This research has been possible thanks to funding from the Centre d'Estudis i de Recerca d'Humanitats (CERHUM) at the Universitat Autònoma de Barcelona, the European Union ERDF Programme and the Spanish Ministry of Education and Science (Research Project ECO2011-29558-C02-01-E) and the Catalan Autonomous Government/Agència de Gestió d'Ajuts Universitaris i de Recerca (AGAUR) (Grant 2014-SGR-502).

References

Calabi-Limentani, I. (1958) *Studi sulla societá romana. Il lavoro artistico*. Milan: Instituto Editoriale Cisalpino. ISBN: 88-2050-305-0.

Izzo, U. (2002). Alle radici della diversità tra copyright e diritto d'autore. In Caso, R., & Pascuzzi, G. (Eds.). *I diritti sulle opere digitali*. Padua: Editorial CEDAM. ISBN: 88-13-24306-5.

Marandola, M. (1998) *Diritto d'autore*. Rome: Associazione Italiana Biblioteche. ISBN: 88-7812-033-2.

Padrós, C., & López-Sintas, J. (2011) *El canon digital a debate. Revolución tecnológica y consumo cultural en un nuevo marco jurídico-económico*. Barcelona: Editorial Atelier. ISBN: 978-84-15929-46-8.

Patterson, L.R. (1968) *Copyright in historical perspective*. Nashville: Vanderbilt University Press. ISBN: 0-8265-1373-5.

Rodríguez-Pardo, J. (2003) *El derecho de autor en la obra multimedia*. Madrid: Editorial Dykinson SL. ISBN: 84-9772-010-5.

Rogel, C. (1984) *Autores, coautores y propiedad intelectual*. Madrid: Editorial Tecnos. ISBN: 8429017364.

Sábada, Í. (2008) *Propiedad Intelectual (bienes públicos o mercancías privadas)*. Madrid: Editorial Catarata. ISBN: 978-84-8319-382-2.

Saunders, D. (1992) *Authorship and copyright*. London: Routledge. ISBN: 9780415041584.

Vega-Vega, J.A. (1990) *Derechos de autor*. Madrid: Editorial Tecnos. ISBN: 84-290-1381-4.

Chapter 3

The current Spanish intellectual property regime: The missing government syndrome?*

Carlos Padrós-Reig

Universitat Autònoma de Barcelona, Spain.
carlos.padros@uab.cat

Doi: http://dx.doi.org/10.3926/oms.300

> **How to cite this chapter**
>
> Padrós-Reig, C. (2015). The current Spanish intellectual property regime: The missing government syndrome? In López-Sintas, J. (Ed.). *The social construction of culture markets: Between incentives to creation and access to culture*. Barcelona, Spain: OmniaScience. pp. 59-99.

---

* This chapter is an updated and shortened version of a chapter published in Spanish in Carlos Padrós-Reig and Jordi López-Sintas (Eds.), (2011). *El Canon Digital a Debate. Revolución Tecnológica y Consumo Cultural en un Nuevo Marco Jurídico-Económico* (Chapter 5, pp. 169-246), reproduced with kind permission from Atelier Editorial (Barcelona).

Abstract

This chapter explores how several issues relating to the digital copying of artistic works have been delineated by recent court judgments in Spain that declare both the automatic calculation of levies and presumptions regarding the use of electronic devices to be unlawful. The Spanish context has also been one of minimal government involvement in defending the public interest. In 2014 the Intellectual Property Commission (CPI) was modified to ensure that the public interest would be better taken into account in determining economic compensation of collective rights. Furthermore, the private method of fee collection has been eliminated, with compensation for public use of artistic works now included as an item in the General State Budget.

This legislative evolution, in a civil law system based on the calculation of damages and on compensation exclusively for right holders, has arrived to the point of distinguishing between private copying and public reproduction. What is evident is the need to take into account the public interest in meeting the challenge of legally adapting to new societal and consumption patterns.

Keywords
Intellectual property, collective rights, Spanish IP law.

1. Context[1]

Conventional wisdom describes the "missing mother syndrome" as a pathology caused by early childhood abandonment or rejection by one's mother. Growing up without the secure presence of a loving, supportive mother is a devastating experience since the mother is the first and basic caretaker. This metaphor can be applied to the malfunctioning Spanish intellectual property (IP) legal regime, given that the public administration (as represented by the Ministry of Culture) — and government in general — has shown a lack of interest in protecting and defending the public interest in terms of accessing culture and remunerating creators.

In our changing world, the digital consumption of culture raises the matter of public use of songs, audiovisual material and other artistic content. It is not merely a question of prosecuting illegal practices but also one of meeting the challenge of legally adapting to new societal and consumption patterns. Of course we are not so naïve as to think that all digital consumption of culture is well meaning. But the fact that the digital revolution has changed the way we access music, literature and films should be accompanied by a deeper reflection on government's role in defending the public interest.

Contemporary transformations in how culture is consumed affect not only production and distribution models but also legal institutions and regulations. It would seem logical that regulations governing IP and private copying should be different in the analogue and digital worlds. In other words, any transformation in how culture is accessed and consumed should be reflected in an updated IP regime.

This article explores the legal nature of private copying and the position of the Spanish public administration regarding this matter. It is evident is that not only has the legislation been poorly adapted to the new technologies, but also that the public administration has largely remained on the sidelines. If fair compensation for private copying responds to a public interest (collective remuneration of authors), then the administration needs to play a greater role

---

1 All translations of excerpts from Spanish regulations, case law and institutional texts and of citations from untranslated works are by Ailish Maher.

in determining both the amount of compensation and how this is collected. In Spain, both efforts to adapt the legislation and the little involvement government regarding IP leave a great deal to be desired.

Generally speaking, legal IP regimes in the 21st century need to deal with two phenomena regarding cultural creation: dematerialization and disintermediation. People can nowadays access artistic works without necessarily using any kind of physical support during consumption and the separation and the steps between production, distribution and consumption of artistic works have all but vanished. What shape should an IP regime adopt in this new context?

Any legal ownership regime governing intellectual and material property is greatly determined by the circumstances of each time and place. It is therefore quite wrong to fossilize the concept of ownership according to standards that no longer exist. In Roman civil law, property was the right to use and abuse what was one's own; in contrast, in the social-democratic state, property is subject to the public interest, which means that antisocial use is prohibited. Since the right to property is a variable and non-absolute social construct, IP should logically be properly adapted to our new technological paradigm.

The same is true of the dividing line between private property and public domain. The subjective constitutional right of access to culture as part of the integral development of persons is considered worthy of protection against the exclusivity of certain forms of trade in culture (e.g., traditional music). Contemplating a painting in a museum cannot be regarded as a taxable act of cultural consumption but as the collective enjoyment of an artistic creation. Similarly, certain types of musical and audiovisual reproduction should also belong to the public cultural domain.

Such notions are contrary to the traditional system for remunerating creators, whose economic rights are traditionally divided into those of an individual nature (contractual) and those of a collective nature (reproduction) acknowledging the creator's rights to fair compensation for private copying. Individual economic rights are easily quantifiable since they are based on a percentage of sales (royalties). Collective economic rights are calculated — on the basis of an estimate of how many copies may be made (e.g., of a book or CD) — by collecting societies as fees raised through a levy applied to devices that could potentially be used to copy and store protected content. Such a levy, which acts in defence of the public interest, goes beyond any strictly private relationship between creator and consumer. Thus, while individual economic rights are agreed privately, compensation for private copying is a public matter.

Directive 2001/29/EC of the European Parliament and of the Council of 22 May 2001 on the harmonization of certain aspects of copyright and related rights in the information society[2] — along with six other directives — establishes the legal basis for copyright in the European Union (EU). This Directive represents the response of the EU legislator to information technology advances that offer right holders new production and exploitation possibilities while creating new challenges for IP protection, given the risk of unauthorized reproduction, imitation or counterfeiting of protected works and content. The Directive also aims to satisfy a legitimate public interest in terms of accessing protected works and content. It is consequently the outcome of the efforts of the EU legislator to reconcile the interests of right holders and the public interest.

Although Article 5.2.b) of this Directive refers only very briefly to private non-commercial copying, Recital 38 states, in greater detail, that the exception for private copying:

> ... may include the introduction or continuation of remuneration schemes to compensate for the prejudice to right holders. Although differences between those remuneration schemes affect the functioning of the internal market, those differences, with respect to analogue private reproduction, should not have a significant impact on the development of the information society. Digital private copying is likely to be more widespread and have a greater economic impact. Due account should therefore be taken of the differences between digital and analogue

---

[2] Available at: http://eur-lex.europa.eu/legal-content/EN/TXT/PDF/?uri=CELEX:32001L0029&from=EN

private copying and a distinction should be made in certain respects between them.

Moreover, according to Recital 45, exceptions and limitations regulated by the member states in accordance with this directive:

...should not (...) prevent the definition of contractual relations designed to ensure fair compensation for the right holders insofar as permitted by national law.

But beyond such general statements of the Preamble, Article 5.2 provides that:

Member States may provide for exceptions or limitations to the reproduction right provided for in Article 2 in the following cases:

(a) in respect of reproductions on paper or any similar medium, effected by the use of any kind of photographic technique or by some other process having similar effects, with the exception of sheet music, provided that the right holders receive fair compensation;

(b) in respect of reproductions on any medium made by a natural person for private use and for ends that are neither directly nor indirectly commercial, on condition that the right holders receive fair compensation which takes account of the application or non-application of technological measures referred to in Article 6 to the work or subject matter concerned.

Given the rejection of a proposed draft directive on private copying presented in 1992, EU harmonization has largely been limited to permitting member states to provide for private copying exceptions. Directive 2001/29/EC, however, effectively prevents member states from allowing any private copying exceptions in their legislation unless some form of remuneration is established. This provision particularly affects countries ruled by the Anglo-Saxon tradition of "fair use" or "fair dealing", which, in specific circumstances, allows private copying with no requirement for remuneration.

Directive 2001/29/EC gives full freedom to member states to determine which devices will be levied (recording equipment, support media or both) and to what extent (according to storage capacity or according to ease of reproduction) and also to determine how to share revenues raised from fees between beneficiaries. There is little EU clarity regarding the issue, however. To cite one of Spain's top legal experts (Garrote, 2007):

> Therefore, for example, perfectly consistent with the Directive is a system of fair compensation (such as the French system) that only considers recording media, but not recording equipment. Also possible is the adoption of a system of legal licensing, such that, for each reproduction for private use, a certain sum is paid to the right holders (as happens in Holland with reprographic copying). It is even possible, when a member state recognizes certain marginal cases of private copying (as in the UK and Ireland with broadcast recordings), that, rather than establish a remuneration scheme, maximum limits be set based on an open system of fair use or fair dealing. The only provision member state legislators cannot overrule is Article 5.5 of Directive 2001/29/EC, which definitively binds them. This flexibility in the system established by the Directive also affects the question of who should be the creditors and debtors of fair compensation and whether there should be mandatory collective rights management. Each state itself must identify, in accordance with its national legislation, the right holders who must be compensated for private copying and to what extent. Finally, flexibility also extends to the method of setting fair compensation. This can be done directly by law (as has been done in Germany, Italy and Portugal) or according to general legal guidelines and a specialized administrative body entrusted with the tasks of fixing the fees payable by creditors and deciding the supports and/or recording equipment subject to compensation (as in France). The matter could also be delegated to an arbitration committee of independent experts or could simply be left to specific agreements between societies representing debtors and creditors. Finally, also possible is a mix of all

these procedures, distinguishing between analogue and digital environments, as has been done in Spain.

While acknowledging that recitals are not the core part of a legal text, there is little doubt regarding their interpretative value in Directive 2001/29/EC, in that they shed more light on the matter in hand. For instance, Recital 35 states:

> In certain cases of exceptions or limitations, right holders should receive fair compensation to compensate them adequately for the use made of their protected works or other subject matter. When determining the form, detailed arrangements and possible level of such fair compensation, account should be taken of the particular circumstances of each case. When evaluating these circumstances, a valuable criterion would be the possible harm to the right holders resulting from the law in question. In cases where right holders have already received payment in some other form, for instance as part of a licence fee, no specific or separate payment may be due. The level of fair compensation should take full account of the degree of use of technological protection measures referred to in this directive. In certain situations where the prejudice to the right holder would be minimal, no obligation for payment may arise.

Against this background of EU regulation, the Spanish system of IP protection is in a state of constant flux as it seeks, in a new technological context, to strike a social and economic balance that takes into account both the rights of creators to remuneration for their work and the rights of individuals to access culture.

This present article, which highlights recent developments in the evolution of the Spanish legal framework, is particularly critical of the lack of involvement of the public administration in matters affecting the public interest. As commented earlier, the cultural consumer's payment of compensation does not represent a private exploitation agreement (license) but a form of tax on a collective good — hence the greater need for a public body to manage this aspect of IP.[3]

2. Legal and Jurisprudential Delimitation of the IP Concept

2.1. High Court Ruling of 22 March 2011: Appeal 704/2008[4]

In 2008 the digital copying levy was normatively implemented by Order PRE/1743/2008 of 18 June. In several simultaneous lawsuits, the High Court considered whether this regulation was lawful. The specific issue in question was the lack of economic dossiers (which must accompany any administrative regulation) detailing how the actual amounts to be levied were to be calculated. This was a purely procedural claim.

Law 23/2006 of 7 July, amending the Consolidated Text of the Intellectual Property Law, approved by Royal Legislative Decree No. 1/1996 of April 12, 1996 (hereafter the LPI) provides some general guidelines. Garrote (2006) analyses in great detail the seven criteria used for drawing up the list of recording equipment and media devices established under Law 23/2006 (Article 25.6 (4)).

> The first of these criteria is the harm actually caused to right holders by private copying. This law adds something that is already contained in Recital 35 of Directive 2001/29/EC, namely that "in certain situations where the prejudice to the right holder would be minimal, no obligation for payment may arise".

This "minimum prejudice rule" can be used to exclude several digital devices and support media which do not, in fact, prejudice right holders because they are not used to make copies for private use. The practical problem is, however, that along with the reproduction function, some digital

---

3 See the World Intellectual Property Organization (WIPO) for a list of Spanish laws and regulations governing IP: http://www.wipo.int/wipolex/en/profile.jsp?code=es#a7.

4 Available from the CENDOJ database: CENDOJ ID 28079230032011100206.

storage space is almost always included in such devices. Hence, several such devices may not be considered as "recording equipment" given that their use for private copying causes minimal prejudice. On the other hand, given that they have a digital memory, they are strong candidates to be included in the list of digital "support media". Garrote (2006) continues as follows:

> The second relevant criterion is the degree of use of equipment or support media for private copying purposes — an attempt to combine the criterion of idoneity with the criterion of "actual use" of the specific equipment or support medium, much discussed during the parliamentary debate (...). Like the previous criterion, this serves to either exclude specific devices or support media from the list or to reduce the amount payable if these are not extensively used in practice to make private copies — as was the case with Spanish Royal Decree 1434/1992 of 27 November, Article 15.2a), whereby aircraft black boxes and answering machines were not considered to be "sound reproduction equipment" for payment purposes.
>
> The third criterion is the storage capacity of equipment and support media, measured in computer storage units (megabyte, gigabyte, terabyte, etc). However, it is not mandatory to establish a recording capacity-to-hours conversion formula, which (...) is extremely important in practice. The only obligation according to this criterion is that a support medium of 1 gigabyte (for instance) should not be liable for more compensation than a support medium of just 500 MB.
>
> The fourth criterion concerns the quality of the copies. Since it is impossible to know copy quality in advance, the regulation must logically consider the equipment. Thus, for example, a DVD recorder capable of making high-definition copies would be liable to pay greater compensation than a lower-end DVD recorder. This is, in short, a matter of higher levies on higher-end products.
>
> The fifth criterion is that the availability, level of application and effectiveness of technological measures must be taken into account, in

line with Articles 31.2 and 161. This requires taking into account the degree of market penetration of such technological measures (mainly anti-copying devices). If technological protection is very robust and there are few private copies in the market (possibly measured by statistical indices), the amount of compensation would have to be significantly reduced. It may even happen that a device or support medium (e.g., a new generation console) incorporates an anti-copying system so effective that private copying or storage in its digital memory would be virtually impossible. Such devices or support media should surely not be obliged to pay compensation.

The sixth criterion is the shelf life of the reproductions, a criterion that logically applies to support media. It seems that this could only be relevant to support media that include some kind of "auto-delete" or "self-destruct" mechanism for stored copies, given that actual conservation of copies depends on environmental conditions and so cannot be taken into account in legislation.

The final criterion is that the amount of compensation applicable to recording equipment and support media should be proportional to the final average retail price — a vague and difficult-to-interpret criterion that was the subject of much discussion during the parliamentary debate. It seems to mean that there should not be excessive disproportion between the final price and the amount of compensation. In practice this will simply serve as a cap or ceiling on the amount of compensation, in that this may not equal or exceed the cost of manufacture.

The list of criteria does not resolve the question of what happens when a digital reproduction device is also a material storage medium (e.g., a DVD recorder with hard-drive storage). It would seem that this kind of equipment should pay compensation both in respect of the device itself (per recording unit) and in respect of its storage capacity (per byte).

Nonetheless, meeting the above criteria was not sufficient to ensure the legality of Order PRE/1743/2008. The High Court Ruling of 22 March 2011 (Appeal 704/2008) found as follows:

> In the case under consideration, the required dossiers are missing and, in their absence, the explanatory note of the draft order in the administrative file cannot be considered a valid replacement. Said note does not effectively meet the requirements regarding dossiers, neither in terms of content nor in the period for which it was produced (after the first negotiation phase for drawing up the Order ended without consensus and before submission to the Council of Consumers and Users [Consejo de Consumidores y Usuarios]).
>
> A corollary to the foregoing is that the omission of the mandatory State Council Opinion and of the mandatory dossiers constitutes a fundamental defect that affects Order PRE/1743/2008 in its entirety, thereby rendering it null and void by law ex article 62.2 of Law 30/1992. Hence, in the case under consideration, it is not incumbent on us to study the grounds, as outlined in the lawsuit, that question the specific regulations described in the Order, whose analysis, furthermore, is not necessary to justify the declaration of nullity that has been anticipated above. Consequently, the fact that the substantive issue remains on the margins of this ruling is sufficient justification for refusing to discuss the question of unconstitutionality raised by the claimant, who failed, in any case, to sufficiently justify his proposal.
>
> We consequently uphold the appeal, but only partially, bearing in mind that this chamber has no knowledge of the aims of the claimant in relation to the retroactive scope of the nullity of the repealed Order regarding the collection of abusive fees and the cessation of indiscriminate charging of fair compensation. This is for the simple reason that fair compensation is a private legal matter and the above petition is consequently outside the jurisdiction of this court. For this

reason, our ruling is limited to declaring the Order under appeal to be null and void.

2.2. Supreme Court Ruling of 13 December 2010: Appeal 1699/2006[5]

This ruling included a discussion of the need for fair compensation to be based on equitable criteria rather than on the automatic application of a percentage of revenues. The first argument of importance was an analysis of the public administration's stance in relation to collecting societies:

The position adopted in the sentence under appeal is not acceptable, in the sense of being obliged to use the general fees notified by collecting societies to the Ministry of Culture in accordance with Article 159.3 of the LPI (...), given that the public administration has not objected for the reason that the LPI has not awarded it fee approval powers but merely the authority to receive notification of these fees (Article 159.3 of the LPI) and, broadly (Article 159.1 of the LPI), a generic oversight role in ensuring compliance with obligations and other requirements established by law. This implies a very minor degree of control that is insufficient to consider that powers to review the fairness of fees correspond exclusively to the public administration and the contentious-administrative jurisdiction.

Moreover, the existence of a prior negotiation process does not guarantee that the general fees meet with the requirements for fairness implied in the very concept of equitable remuneration, as expressed, in relation to the case under consideration, in Article 108.3 of the LPI (now Article 108.5).

Otherwise, the impossibility of reaching agreement in the negotiation phase would automatically entail the possibility, contrary to the law, that collecting societies could unilaterally set general fees, even if said fees were not fair.

---

5   Available from the CENDOJ database: CENDOJ ID 28079110012010100854.

The second argument of relevance is an analysis of the specific criteria for calculating fees (quantification of fair compensation):

The appellant posits, in an allegation that is not rejected by the appellee, that the general fees are set exclusively according to the claimant company's turnover. This cannot be accepted in absolute terms. As was made clear in the Supreme Court Ruling of 21 January 2009 it is clear that the criterion of actual use of the repertoire — insofar as this can be applied — is fairer than the criterion of availability or of quantification according to company turnover.

Another criterion that must be taken into account, as expressly stated by the appellant, is that of a comparison with agreements between collecting societies and other production companies, given that fairness is closely related to the requirement that fees for different production companies be similar. This is not to say that they must be identical, rather that there should be no excessive disproportion that cannot be justified for management or other reasons.

In the Supreme Court Ruling of 22 December 2008, this court declared null and void any agreement with a production company based on an unjustified lack of proportion regarding fees subsequently approved in an agreement with another association.

The appellee seems to justify charging what appear to be more onerous fees for the defendant than for other production companies, based on the fact of the defendant having rejected the other fees offered during the negotiation phase. It is clear, however, that not having reached agreement during a negotiation process is not in itself a justification for the imposition of more onerous fees than objectively respond to fairness criteria weighted in terms of fees applied to other bodies in the corresponding agreements. This would place one negotiating party in a position of superiority and in a position to impose his will on the other party, thereby ensuring that agreement content would be as dictated by him.

It must also be borne in mind that the LPI relates the obligation of companies to set general fees to the use of a repertoire (Article 152.1b). What this means is that, in setting fees, consideration must be given to criteria associated with the extent of the repertoires (of collecting societies in comparison with each other) and with right holders due fair compensation. These right holders are not just those who have entered into management agreements with collecting societies, but also others outside the compensation distribution mechanisms operated by one or all of the collecting societies.

The Supreme Court finally arrived at a doctrinal conclusion:

In relation to author rights arising from public communication of audiovisual works, the jurisprudence of this chamber has already implicitly stated that, irrespective of the circumstances of the negotiation, fair compensation cannot be established in an unconditional fashion according to general fees established unilaterally by collecting societies, not even when these fees may have been approved by the public administration. Rather, various criteria have been considered that align fair compensation with actual use principles that themselves guarantee fairness. Indeed, the Supreme Court Ruling of 20 September 2007 states that "it is not disputed that the claimant has applied the established fees and that these fees have been set in accordance with a legal rule; this does not preclude their being called into question, however, even though in this case there has been no disagreement or record of conflict in regard to abusive or unfair charges."

Supreme Court Ruling of 15 January 2008, in referring to fair compensation for producers of audiovisual works for public TV broadcasts in hotels, declares that "the appropriate price for public communication already considered as such must be determined according to two criteria: the management body agreement, in this case with the respondent hotel or, as more usually occurs, with a hotel association; or, in the absence of an agreement of this type, the price ostensibly established by the fee structure notified by the collecting society to the Ministry of Culture (...). This is not to say that said fees must prevail in the face of any opposition from those obliged to pay, as the law requires that fees must be subject to the criterion of fairness. Fairness as outlined in Article 3.2 of the Civil Code requires prudent and restrictive consideration (Supreme Court Ruling of 8 February 1996)."

As stated in the Ruling of 15 July 1985, while Article 3.2 of the Civil Code prohibits the exclusive use of fairness as grounds for rulings unless clearly authorized, it does not prohibit fair weighting in regard to application of rules, which is the case that concerns us here (Supreme Court Ruling of 15 March 1995). The rulings of 12 June 1990, 11 October 1988 and 3 November 1987 are based on the same reasoning. And, in regard to the case under consideration, the ruling adds that "the application of the established fees cannot reasonably be deemed abusive, in the absence of any agreement, when applied to a real use of public communication, that is, in 'occupied' rooms and apartments. A different view would be taken of a claim for indemnification that was based on a calculation of the total 'available' rooms or apartments."

The plea is consequently upheld, since the requirement for fairness in setting fair compensation based on collecting societies fees must be subject to oversight by the courts, and therefore — following the doctrine established in the Supreme Court Ruling of 7 April 2009, which resolved an appeal very similar to this one — the appellant's petition must be partially admitted. It is hereby declared, in enforcement of the ruling, that fair compensation must be determined, according to the general fees notified by the AIE [Spanish Society of Artistic Performers] to the public administration, by fairly weighting the fees resulting from the defendant's income and taking into account, among other factors indicative of the extent of the repertoire, actual use, financial volume of operations and the existence of agreements with other companies involved in public communication activities.

2.3. Supreme Court Ruling of 6 June 2011 (CEDRO Case): Appeal 837/2007[6]

In what became known as the CEDRO case — referring to the Spanish Reprographic Rights Centre (Centro Español de Derechos Reprográficos, CEDRO) — the claimant had made photocopies in an establishment open to the public without prior authorization by the copyright holder. An appeal in cassation was upheld and the original judgment reversed (the claimant was ordered to pay ten times the full amount of the fees he would have had to pay had he obtained authorization).

The contested sentence was declared to contravene legal doctrine established regarding the setting of compensation according to Article 140 of the LPI. Had reproduction been authorized, compensation would have amounted to the general fees established for authorized copying of 10% of a work, multiplied by five. Specifically, the ruling stated as follows:

1. We declare that there are grounds for the appeal in cassation (...) against the ruling issued on appeal — Proceedings 18/2007 — by the Provincial Court of Valencia, Section 9, on 22 February 2007, which stated as follows:

"While upholding, in part, the appeal submitted by CEDRO's legal representative against the ruling of 26 October 2006 of Mercantile Court 2 of Valencia (...), we hereby partially revoke said ruling, and, for the reasons outlined above, the defendant is ordered, in the terms outlined in the first-instance ruling, to apply the fees, multiplied by ten, that would have applied had the requisite authorization been obtained in the period in question and bearing in mind the revoked ruling. The remaining pleas of the judgment under appeal are upheld, including the non-imposition of costs for the proceedings at first instance, due to the underlying legal doubts. There will be no award of costs regarding this appeal."

2. We annul the ruling, which we hereby declare to be null and void.

---

6   Available from the CENDOJ database: CENDOJ ID 28079110012011100432.

3. Instead, while partially upholding the appeal submitted by CEDRO's legal representative against the ruling of 26 October 2006 of Mercantile Court 2 of Valencia (...), we hereby partially revoke said ruling, and, for the reasons outlined above, the defendant is ordered, in the terms outlined in the first-instance ruling, to apply the fees, multiplied by five, that would have applied had the requisite authorization been obtained in the period in question and bearing in mind the revoked ruling. The remaining pleas of the judgment under appeal are upheld, with non-imposition of costs for the proceedings at first instance.

4. The following legal doctrine is reiterated: the compensation required under Article 140 of the LPI for unauthorized photocopying in establishments open to the public — in accordance with the general fee schedule for the claimant CEDRO and the compensation that would have been received had the required authorization been obtained — must be calculated as the amount of the general fee for authorized copies of 10% of a work, multiplied by five. If it can be adequately proven that the average percentage of photocopies of the work was less or more than 50%, the fee may be multiplied by a higher or lower coefficient, to a maximum of ten times the amount.

The CEDRO case thus resulted in legal doctrine that disallows the presumption that copying was authorized. Furthermore, the Supreme Court had declared a year earlier that fair compensation needed to be based on equitable criteria and not on the automatic application of a percentage of revenues. Finally, the declaration of invalidity of Order PRE/1743/2008 launched a debate regarding how to calculate fair compensation for private copying in Spain — a debate which also had the outcome of leading to a questioning of IP regulation in more general terms. It was becoming clear that fair compensation could not be established in an unconditional manner according to general fees established unilaterally by collecting societies, even when these fees had been approved by the public administration.

To sum up, these three cases of court judgments invalidating the IP system led to a general questioning regarding the calculation and levying of copying fees and a broad consensus that legal reforms were critical.

3. The Intellectual Property Commission (CPI)

A public administrative structure with regulatory and oversight powers must obviously play a key role in IP matters. Establishing, collecting and managing a private copying levy is, much like a duty or tax, a matter of public interest. Regulation of the Intellectual Property Commission (Comisión de la Propiedad Intelectual, CPI, formerly called the Intellectual Property Mediation and Arbitration Commission) and of the powers of the Ministry of Culture was originally addressed in Articles 158 and 159 of the LPI, as follows:

Article 158. Intellectual Property Mediation and Arbitration Commission

An Intellectual Property Mediation and Arbitration Commission is hereby created, as a national collegiate body, in the Ministry of Culture, with the functions of mediation and arbitration as attributed to it under this law.

1. The Commission will perform its mediation functions by doing the following:

a) Participating in negotiations between parties, provided they have granted their consent, in the event of failure to agree regarding the authorization of cable distribution of television broadcasts in the absence of agreement between intellectual property right holders and cable distribution companies.

b) Where required, making proposals to the parties.

It will be considered that all parties accept the Commission's proposals as outlined in the previous paragraph if they do not expressly state their opposition within three months, in which case, the decision of the Commission will produce the effects outlined in Law 36/1988 of 5 December governing arbitration, with an option for review by the civil courts.

The parties will be informed of the proposal and of any opposition to the same in accordance with Articles 58 and 59 of Law 30/1992 of 26 November governing the legal regime of public administrations and common administrative procedure.

The mediation procedure and the composition of the Commission for the purposes of said mediation will be determined in the regulations. Two representatives from the collecting society representing the intellectual property rights subject to negotiation and two representatives from the cable broadcasting company shall be entitled to participate in the Commission regarding any matter that affects them.

2. The Commission will perform its arbitration functions by doing the following:

a) Resolving, provided the parties have granted their consent, conflicts which, in application of Point 1 of the above article, may arise between collecting societies and associations of users or broadcasters of collecting society repertoires. Submission to the authority of the Commission is voluntary and must be expressed in writing.

b) Setting substitutory amounts for the general fees, for the purpose indicated in Point 2 of the above article, at the request of an association of users or a broadcaster, provided these agree to submit to the authority of the Commission for the purpose outlined in a) above.

3. The procedure and composition of the Commission for the purposes of arbitration shall be established by legislation. Two representatives from the collecting society and two representatives from the association of users or from the broadcasting company shall be entitled to participate in the Commission regarding any matter that affects them.

The decisions of the Commission shall be binding and enforceable.

The contents of this article are without prejudice to any legal action that may be brought in the relevant jurisdiction. However, submission of a conflict to arbitration by the Commission will prevent judges and courts from addressing the matter until the decision of the Commission has been issued and provided that the party invokes the same by way of derogation.

Article 159. Powers of the Ministry of Culture

1. In addition to the power to grant or revoke authorizations as described in Articles 148 and 149, the Ministry of Culture shall have oversight powers regarding compliance with the obligations and requirements described in this law.

[Article 159.1. Paragraph 2. Declared unconstitutional by Constitutional Court Ruling 196/1997 of 13 November].

2. Without prejudice to provisions in other relevant legislation, modifications to the statutes of the collecting societies, once approved by the general assembly of members, must be submitted to the Ministry of Culture for approval, and shall, moreover, be considered as approved if no decision declaring otherwise is notified within three months of submission.

[Article 159.3. Declared unconstitutional by Constitutional Court Ruling 196/1997 of 13 November].

Leaving aside the lack of an implementing regulation regarding the CPI, its ineffectiveness was a clear obstacle to the proper functioning of the IP system. By virtue of Additional Provision 2 of Law 23/2006, the CPI should be a key administrative intervention element regarding IP protection in Spain, most especially in regard to setting fees. Two basic kinds of models were possible:

1. The first option would be for unilaterally set fees, considered as inherent to the public interest, to be managed by collecting societies

authorized by the Ministry of Culture. The collecting societies would be established as corporate administrative bodies — like associations of liberal professionals or sports federations. There should be an absolute and rigorous requirement to defer to the CPI — as happens, for instance, in German law — in matters of economically despotic behaviour.

2. The second option would be to consider collecting societies as subject to market competition rules as apply in any other economic sector. Negotiations with users or with an arbitration commission would be unnecessary, given that competition between collecting societies would establish equitable prices.

According to Delgado-Porras (1995), the first option would constitute an internal contradiction regarding the system established by the legislator to ensure fairness —which is no other than the application of economic competition rules by the courts or by the corresponding administrative bodies.

Nonetheless, there was no evident interaction between the CPI and the aforementioned competition authorities — mainly due to the poor view held of the CPI, there being a clear preference for disputes with collecting societies to be aired in lengthy lawsuits or in administrative (competition law) procedures.

The problem in Spain lay precisely in the mixing of two systems: fees were unilaterally set in a de facto monopoly whose logic was based on collecting societies defending the public interest, yet there was no public control over the setting of these fees.[7] Thus, the legislation regulating IP management encouraged the existence of a quasi-legal monopoly, yet antitrust rules were applied to what was not really a market.

---

7   It is interesting to contrast this fee system with the system established, for instance, for industrial control and inspection tasks implemented by bodies attached to the public administration. In this case, the fee schedule of amounts to be charged in the future must be filed along with the documentation required for accreditation. In other words, for industrial inspection bodies, fees, although private, are subject to certain administrative controls at the time of initial accreditation of the inspection body.

In its Decision of 27 July 2000 regarding Case 465/99, the Spanish Competition Tribunal (Tribunal de Defensa de la Competencia) touched the heart of the matter when it stated as follows (Fact 10):

> The current LPI in practice creates a frustrating vacuum when parties fail to reach agreement regarding what constitutes a fair once-off payment, as it has been considered sufficient to create a commission with powers of voluntary arbitration and mediation. Most likely it was imagined that the seeds of competition would germinate and bloom in the field of intellectual property rights management. However, precisely the opposite has come to pass, namely, the proliferation of monopolies that individually manage multiple recognized rights.[8]

The above declaration made patent the fact that pathways were open in all directions. Either we take compensation fees to be remuneration regarding a matter of public interest overseen by the public administration, or we accept that collecting societies should be deprived of all their prerogatives — used, it may be said in passing, with poor judgement. Perez de Ontiveros-Baquero (1993) has warned that overzealousness in protecting IP rights may even restrict the dissemination of creations, thereby upsetting the balance between IP protection and access to culture:

> ... a single communicative act may require multiple authorizations and may even require the payment of several levies — circumstances that would create such a burden that the economic advantage of using an intellectual creation may be perceived as not worth the disbursement to be made (...) The social vocation of intellectual creations can only be enforced through adequately scaled fees and corrective interpretation of the regulations.

---

[8] Available at http://www.cnmc.es/es-es/competencia/buscadorde/resoluciones.aspx.

The failure of the Ministry of Culture to exercise its control functions regarding the collecting societies and the setting of compensation fees could only be decried as negligent. Rodríguez-Tapia (2007) upbraided the government as follows:

> What is more serious, however, is that neither the government nor the courts have seen fit to materially or substantially remodel the CPI, which, despite good intentions, has proved ineffective, bound hand and foot as it is in terms of playing its true and desirable role of supervising collective management of IP rights. Authors like Rodrigo Bercovitz and Casas Valles have, for years, been calling for reform. This reform cannot wait. Yet Law 23/2006 of 7 July has postponed for another day the reforms it mentions, as its Additional Provision 2 merely authorizes the government to implement regulatory reforms in the future.

The CPI was described by Spanish IP legislation as a collegiate body of national scope with arbitration functions regarding parties and substitutory functions regarding the setting of general fees. With the approval of Law 2/2011 of 4 March on the sustainable economy (LES), the CPI was empowered with the additional function of adopting measures to suspend information society services (i.e., the Internet). The main innovations of the 2011 reforms were as follows:

- CPI division into two sections: Section I, mediation and arbitration, and Section II, safeguarding of IP rights.
- Conferral of powers on Section I to set substitutory fees in the absence of agreement between parties.
- Conferral of powers on Section II to punish infringement of IP rights.
- Conferral of powers on the contentious-administrative courts to authorize suspension of information society services in the event of infringement.

The CPI was thus composed as follows:

Section I	President appointed by the government 3 members — persons of recognized expertise in the IP field — nominated by the Ministries of the Economy, Culture and Justice Term of 3 years, renewable once
Section II	Presidency held by the Sub-Secretary of State for Culture 4 members nominated by the Ministries of Culture, the Economy, Industry, Tourism and Trade and the Presidency

The LES, in its Final Provision 43 (popularly called the Sinde Law after the Minister of Culture of the day), described Section II in the following terms:

> Section II, which shall act in accordance with the principles of objectivity and proportionality, will be responsible for exercising the functions provided for in Articles 8 and related articles of Law 34/2002, aimed at safeguarding intellectual property rights against infringement by providers of information society services. The Section may adopt measures to suspend the provision of an information society service that infringes intellectual property rights and to remove content that infringes these rights, provided that the provider, directly or indirectly, acts with a profit motive or has caused or is likely to harm ownership rights. Prior to the adoption of these measures, the information society service provider shall be issued with a formal request to proceed, within a period not exceeding 48 hours, with the voluntary removal of the infringing content or, if applicable, to make claims and provide suitable evidence concerning authorized use or the applicability of a limit to the intellectual property right. Once the above deadline has passed, where necessary, evidence will be examined within two days and will be forwarded to interested parties for conclusions within five days. The Commission shall then issue a decision within a maximum of three days. Voluntary withdrawal of the infringing content shall halt the proceedings. Implementation of the measure, in the event of non-compliance with the formal request, shall require prior judicial

authorization, in accordance with the procedure described in Article 122 bis, Point 2, of the law governing the contentious-administrative jurisdiction.

3.1. Development of New Legislation

The legal configuration of the new CPI was normatively implemented by Royal Decree 1889/2011 of 30 December governing the functioning of the CPI. The draft submitted for consultation to the General Council of the Judiciary (Consejo General del Poder Judicial, CGPJ)[9] merited an Opinion[10] that is of undoubted interest here:

ONE. With regard to the composition and legal system governing CPI Sections I and II:

– In appointing members of Section I, the principle of regulatory hierarchy is possibly contravened by Article 3.1 of the draft, in terms of the inclusion of the evaluation of certain requirements of experience and knowledge not provided for in the LPI.

– Note that the appointment of the President of Section I must be by joint Ministerial Order, and not by means of a "joint proposal" of the Ministry of Culture and the Ministry of the Economy (Article 158.3.4 of the LPI).

– Note, regarding substitution of the President of Section I, a possible contradiction between Article 3.2 "in fine" and Article 3.4 of the draft.

– It is recommended that the assignation to the secretary of the oversight role regarding the independence, neutrality and impartiality of Section I be revised.

---

9   Procedural rules for the approval of Royal Decrees make it compulsory to consult the CGPJ whose opinion is non-binding but is usually taken into account since it may prevent future litigation.

10 Available at http://www.poderjudicial.es/stfls/cgpj/COMISI%C3%93N%20DE%20ESTUDIOS%20E%20INFORMES/INFORMES%20DE%20LEY/DOCUMENTOSCGPJ/021%2011.pdf.

– It is recommended that further thought be given to the asymmetry regarding eligibility requirements for members of the two Sections.

– Various observations are made regarding the description of the legal regime applicable to Section II.

TWO. In relation to mediation procedures before CPI Section I.

– A possible contradiction is observed between the possibility of one party requesting mediation and the legal requirement that the CPI acts as a mediator "provided both parties have granted their consent".

– It is recommended to add the qualification "where required" in the passage referring to the CPI's formulation of a proposed solution to a conflict in Article 6.3 of the draft.

– The solution proposed by the Commission should not have the requirement to be motivated, whereas there should be a requirement for motivation when the CPI decides to put an end to the proceedings on considering agreement between the parties to be impossible. Likewise, motivation should be a requirement for parties refusing to accept the solution proposed by the Commission.

– It is recommended, in the interest of legal certainty and to avoid abuse, to set a maximum period for the mediation proceedings after which there can be no more attempts to reach agreement.

– It would be appropriate for the draft to include a statement regarding legal or extra-judicial actions while the mediation process is under way.

THREE. With regard to potential compatibility between mediation and arbitration proceedings before CPI Section I:

– It is suggested that some mechanism be set up to establish precedence for proceedings, in the event that these are requested at the same time by the parties in conflict.

– In order to avoid disparate outcomes, a system needs to be established to channel issues through a single procedure to avoid different parties on the same side of a conflict submitting simultaneous requests for mediation or arbitration to the CPI.

FOUR. In relation to arbitration proceedings before CPI Section I:

– So as not to pervert the essentially voluntary nature of arbitration and so possibly undermine the right to effective legal protection, it is recommended that Article 2.3 of the draft or its first subsection be removed. At the very least, we suggest that the term "unjustified" be removed.

– Note that supplementary application of the Arbitration Law will affect the regime governing the adoption of agreements and the Presidential planning, processing and promotion functions, as the draft regulation may unintentionally force these to be processed in other terms.

– It is recommended, to avoid any possible delays, that a maximum time frame for the proceedings be established that is more in keeping with Article 37.2 of the Arbitration Law. It is also suggested that arbitrators be permitted to resolve disputes by declaring one or more arbitral awards.[11]

Even though the CGPJ pointed out several technical errors in the wording of the CPI regulation, Royal Decree 1889/2011 of 30 December largely met with approval. Its main content is described in the following paragraphs.

Royal Decree 1889/2011 regulates the functioning of the CPI as a national collegiate body attached to the Ministry of Culture and regulated by the LPI. As we have noted, the LES (Final Provision 43, i.e., the Sinde Act) profoundly changed the CPI in that its functions of mediation and arbitration were broadened and actions aimed at safeguarding IP rights were added, thus conferring the body with more peremptory powers.

---

11 Text available at http://www.poderjudicial.es/stfls/cgpj/COMISI%C3%93N%20DE%20ESTUDIOS%20E%20INFORMES/INFORMES%20DE%20LEY/DOCUMENTOSCGPJ/021%2011.pdf.

The CPI continues to be divided into two sections. Section I, responsible for mediation and arbitration, has had its material scope greatly broadened. This reinforcement of its role makes it the ideal instrument for settling disputes in the current IP system. Section II, meanwhile, exercises the new function of safeguarding IP rights against infringement by providers of information society services. A mixed administrative and judicial procedure has been established to safeguard fundamental rights that requires the intervention of the Central Contentious-Administrative Court.

Regarding Section I, mediation powers extend to all matters directly related to the collective management of IP rights, whereas arbitration powers extend to conflicts between collecting societies, between right holders and collecting societies and between broadcasters and collecting societies. Also important is its arbitration function and its powers to set substitutory fees. Section I is thus converted, in the existing IP system, into the ideal instrument for non-judicial conflict resolution, provided that the parties voluntarily agreed to submit to its decisions.

As for Section II, its main function is to safeguard IP rights against infringement by Internet service providers. The procedures described in the legal text are thus not directed against users, but against service providers infringing IP rights by offering or intermediating in illegal content. A core requirement is that, directly or indirectly, a profit motive exists or financial loss or harm is caused — or likely to be caused — to the right holder. The goal is to remove any obstacle to the full exercise of IP rights and to restore legality when rights have been infringed, for which purpose, a service may be suspended or infringing content may be removed.

Royal Decree 1889/2011 of 30 December regulates administrative procedures but also provides for Central Contentious-Administrative Court intervention, at the behest of the CPI, in two specific circumstances:

- When holders of infringed rights who have initiated proceedings cannot identify those responsible for the infringement, they may request the Central Contentious-Administrative Court to issue a formal request, to the provider of intermediation services, regarding the data necessary to

> identify and locate the infringers. Under this procedure, the right of access to this information enables civil and criminal actions to be pursued if necessary.

- When the existence of an infringement of IP rights has been proven and content removal or service interruption has been ordered, if those responsible do not willingly comply within 24 hours, the Central Contentious-Administrative Court may be requested to force compliance within three days of enforcement of the order.

These mechanisms enable rapid decisions in resolving rights infringements. Deadlines for both the administrative and judicial phases are very short and the administrative procedure allows for the use of electronic communications.

The regulatory implementation of the CPI was published in the Official State Gazette (Boletín Oficial del Estado, BOE) of 31 December 2011, simultaneously with Royal Decree Law 20/2011 of 30 December (governing urgent budgetary, tax and financial measures for the correction of the public deficit), which has an Additional Provision worded as follows:

Additional Provision 10. Modification of the fair compensation regime for private copying.

1. Hereby abolished is fair compensation for private copying as provided for in Article 25 of the Consolidated Text of the Intellectual Property Law, approved by Royal Decree 1/1996 of 12 April, with limits as established in Article 31.2 of the same law.

2. The government shall establish by law the procedure for payment of fair compensation for private copying from the General State Budget.

3. The amount of compensation to be paid will be decided based on an estimate of the harm caused.

The digital copying levy was thus abolished, leaving fair compensation for private copying to be charged to the General State Budget. The regulatory mechanism implemented is based on compensation (calculated on the basis of the harm caused to creators) for the fact that private copying remains fully legal. The amount is determined by the public administration following dialogue with the sectors concerned, in full compliance with the regulatory and jurisprudential framework of the EU. In an article published in *El País*, Seisdedos and Fraguas (2011) commented as follows:

> Vice-President Soraya Saenz de Santamaría (...) has announced the replacement of the digital copying levy (...) by a universal tax. So, we will all pay, whether or not we make private copies. According to ministry sources, the compensation, to be agreed with the collecting societies, will be drawn from an item in the General State Budget and will amount to between 37 and 42 million [euros], a figure arrived at by multiplying the Spanish population by 0.8 or 0.9 euros per head. Less than half the amount raised in 2010 from the previous system.

Paradoxically therefore, as soon as the administrative structure designed to regulate the calculation of fees was reformed, the very fee itself was abolished, thereby rendering the whole discussion pointless.

Finally, we conclude this section by referring to Supreme Court Ruling of 31 May 2013 (Appeal 48/2012).[12] Several collecting societies challenged Royal Decree 1889/2011 (Rodríguez-Portugués, 2013), arguing that a purely administrative body had been conferred with powers that restrict fundamental rights. The Court rejected the claim, reasoning as follows (Point of Law 8):

> It is indeed true that fundamental rights are at stake, as indicated by the appellant on citing, essentially, freedom of expression and freedom of information. Nonetheless, the importance of these rights, their nature as necessary elements of a free and pluralistic public opinion and their expression on the Internet — an extraordinary stimulant for culture, leisure, communications and trade — does not preclude administrative intervention in this area, already a tradition in the telecommunications and audiovisual sectors. These fundamental rights, which are not unlimited, do not preclude the creation of an administrative body, the design of an administrative procedure and the adoption of a series of

---

[12] Available from the CENDOJ database: CENDOJ ID 28079130042013100154.

measures aimed at restoring online legality, provided that constitutional and legally established safeguards are respected, and especially bearing in mid that administrative action is subject to review by judges and courts in fulfilment of the oversight role conferred on them by the Spanish Constitution regarding the legality of administrative acts and provisions, ex Article 106.1 of the Spanish Constitution (...). In other words, in many other areas of administrative activity fundamental rights are also at stake to varying degrees. Yet this does not mean that it must be judges who directly implement measures to restore legality. These measures may be implemented by an administrative body like CPI Section II acting in accordance with the principles of objectivity and proportionality (Article 158.4 of the LPI), provided that constitutional and legally established guarantees are respected. Therefore, to suspend an information society service that infringes IP rights or to remove infringing content, an administrative decision is sufficient, provided that it is subject to appropriate procedures that allow a hearing of the affected party, without prejudice to the fact that the implementation of these measures requires judicial authorization, as stated in Articles 9 and 122 bis of the LJCA [Law 29/1998 of 13 July governing the contentious-administrative jurisdiction] as amended by Law 2/2011 of 4 March on the sustainable economy (...). Judicial bodies will rule on the legality of the procedure after the fact, should the proceedings of Section II of the Commission be disputed. Note, finally, that the contested Royal Decree, as also Article 158 of the LPI, indicate that it is the Central Contentious-Administrative Court which must enforce the measure in the event of non-compliance with the formal request, in accordance with the procedure described in the cited Article 122 bis and also included as Final Provision 43.7 of Law 2/2011 of 4 March on the sustainable economy.

In the same Ruling, the option of a strictly judicial regulation was stated to be just one of several possibilities (Point of Law 9):

The general idea of the appellant association is that, to safeguard intellectual property, a different system should have been established in which judicial bodies would be directly responsible for monitoring legality online in the interest of protecting intellectual property, since, in the opinion of the appellant, this system would offer better guarantees. The non-involvement of the public administration in this area is defended, and future intellectual property infringements should be dealt with by the courts. This is one opinion of many legitimate others, although not relevant to the case concerning us here, as that debate, being beyond the scope of this case, cannot be brought into the appeal, and has, indeed, already been resolved in the courts following a different format to that proposed by the appellant. And so, it is not only appropriate but also mandatory that this should — and indeed must — be implemented by law in accordance with the challenged Royal Decree, by virtue of the principle of normative hierarchy, there being no other option (Article 9.3 of the Spanish Constitution). The confluence, essentially, of rights to freedom of expression (Article 20.1.a) of the Spanish Constitution) and of information (Article 20.1.d) of the Spanish Constitution) and, specifically, the right to literary, artistic, scientific and technical production (Article 20.1.b) of the Spanish Constitution), as well as other rights — such as the right to personal and familial privacy (Article 18.4 of the Spanish Constitution) and access to culture, among others — and the limited nature of said rights, all determine the need to take measures that limit their respective scopes and balance them in terms of connections. However, this regulatory configuration should not be disproportionate, nor should it involve any undue restriction on the rights of citizens, nor should the legal regulations as provided for in Article 158 of the LPI raise doubts regarding their constitutionality, as we have already mentioned. Bear in mind that Section II of the Commission exercises, according to Article 158.4 of the LPI, the functions outlined in Article 8 and concurrent articles of Law 34/2002 of 11 July on information society services and electronic commerce, which outline the "measures necessary to suspend provision or remove infringing information", followed by a list of the principles that may be violated by information society services. These include safeguarding public order, investigating crime, ensuring public safety and national defence (part a); protection of public health (part b); respect for personal dignity and the principle of non-discrimination (part c); protection of youth and children (part d); and, of concern to us here, the safeguarding of intellectual property rights (part c)."

3.2. Law 21/2014 of 4 November Amending the LPI

More recent reform of the LPI — popularly called the Lassalle Law after the Secretary of State for Culture of the day — represents a strengthening of ministerial administrative powers regarding enforcement of this legislation (e.g., the new Article 159, covering public administration powers). Although a thorough analysis of the scope of this reform is not possible here, certain references to the CPI are worthy of comment.

In general terms, the concept of fair compensation for private copying has been modified in that the number of cases eligible for compensation is reduced. Also, as mentioned, fair compensation as referred to in Article 31.2 is to be charged annually to the General State Budget, with the procedures for setting and paying compensation fees being those established by law. Furthermore, payment will be made through the collecting societies; this has led to Article 25 of the LPI, referring to fair compensation for private copying, being modified.[13]

Also modified is the article regulating CPI Section I, which has the effect of broadening its powers to include a fee-setting function and strengthening

---

[13] This regulation has been approved — despite the Supreme Court Ruling of 10 September 2014 suspending the contentious-administrative appeal against Royal Decree 1657/2012 of 7 December governing the procedure for payment of compensation for private copying from the General State Budget. The Supreme Court ruling posed two questions concerning interpretation of Directive 2001/29 Article 5.2.b): first, whether compensation via the General State Budget ensures that the cost is borne by actual users of copies; and, second, whether such compensation may be affected by budgetary limits set annually, thereby creating an imbalance between the interests of the right holders and those of the users of the private copies.

its oversight role in ensuring that fees are fair and non-discriminatory. To this end, Article 158 has been amended as follows:

Article 158. Intellectual Property Commission: composition and functions

1. The Intellectual Property Commission (CPI) is hereby created as a collegiate body with national scope affiliated to the Ministry of Culture. It will carry out the functions of mediation, arbitration, fee-setting and oversight in the cases provided for in the present Title, and will safeguard intellectual property rights in accordance with this law. The CPI will also exercise an advisory function with respect to all matters within its scope and regarding which it may be consulted by the Ministry of Culture.

2. The CPI will be formed of two Sections: a) Section I shall exercise all functions of mediation, arbitration, fee-setting and oversight in the cases provided for in the present Title.

b) Section II shall oversee, within the scope marked by the powers of the Ministry of Culture, the safeguarding of intellectual property rights from infringement by information society services, in the terms outlined in Article 8 and related articles of Law 34/2002 of 11 July governing information society services and electronic commerce.

3. Section I shall be formed of four members who may delegate their functions to their respective deputies. All members will be recognized experts in the intellectual property and competition field. The Ministry of Culture shall appoint a president who will hold the casting vote. The members of Section I shall be appointed by government royal decree on the basis of nominations by the Ministers of Culture, the Economy, Justice and Industry, Energy and Tourism. Terms shall run for five years and may be renewed once. The government may legally modify the composition of Section I.

4. The president of Section II shall be the Secretary of State for Culture or a person delegated by him/her. Section II shall be formed of two members from the Ministry of Culture, one from the Ministry of Industry, Energy and Tourism, one from the Ministry of Justice, one from the Ministry of the Economy and one from the Ministry of the Presidency. The members shall be nominated by their respective departments from among public administration staff groups or categories with advanced qualifications and accredited expertise in intellectual property matters. (...) Section II functioning and the procedure for exercising its functions shall be determined by law.

The new CPI is now composed as follows:

Section I	President appointed by the government 3 members — persons of recognized expertise in the IP field — nominated by the Ministries of Culture, the Economy, Justice and Industry, Energy and Tourism Term of 5 years, renewable once
Section II	Presidency held by the Secretary of State for Culture 6 members nominated by the Ministries of Culture, the Economy, Justice. Industry, Energy and Tourism and the Presidency

The mandate of CPI Section I members has been lengthened from three to five years and CPI Section II members now number seven, all appointed by the government,

As regards functions, the amended Article 158 bis (Paragraphs 3, 4 and 5) reinforces the mechanisms for establishing fair and non-discriminatory fees and also provides for the National Markets and Competition Commission (Comisión Nacional de los Mercados y la Competencia, CNMC) to be notified in the event of non-compliance so that it can act accordingly.

Finally, a new Article 158 ter has been added that very wordily details (Paragraphs 3, 4, 5 and 6) the procedures and conditions under which CPI Section II may proceed to suspend information society services that infringe IP rights, with fines of up to €600,000 for failure to remove infringing content.

The quasi-judicial role of the CPI was addressed in State Council Opinion 1064/2013 of 28 November 2013[14] which, in analysing the draft version of Law 21/2014 (see Section 3.2), mainly relied on Supreme Court Ruling of 31 May 2013 (see end of Section 3.1). The State Council Opinion points to the different configurations of a similar body to the CPI in the European setting (Section 7.5.6):

> The continuity of the draft law at this point is in direct contrast with the experience of neighbouring countries where the usual procedure is the creation of ad hoc entities, such as the French HADOPI (...) whose composition involves the highest authorities in the country, ensuring independence and autonomy in the exercise of its functions. This is even more notable when, as is the case here, the draft law amends the functions of the CPI in number and in importance in terms that merely translate into the anticipation of a possible increase in the number of members of Section I. If it is intended, with the attribution of new functions to the CPI, to improve public vigilance of the market for IP rights, then Sections I and II must be provided with the necessary material and human means, it being necessary to determine, with greater precision in the legislation, the subjective requisites for membership of the Sections by persons who must be able exercise the public tasks entrusted to them with suitable knowledge and efficiency.
>
> The above confirms a poorly functioning system of appointments and emphasizes that the important function entrusted to the CPI requires suitable allocation of human and financial resources — for which there is no provision in the legislation. This lack of means may well compromise the future activities of the CPI.

---

14 Available at https://www.boe.es/buscar/doc.php?id=CE-D-2013-1064.

4. Conclusions

The consumption of culture is experiencing a profound paradigmatic shift, due to the new technologies and the emergence of new forms of access to creations and new consumer habits. The legal regime, always reactive to change, finds it difficult to accommodate the new digital scenario.

In 2006, the Consolidated Text of the LPI was reformed with the inclusion of a newly worded Article 25 on fair compensation for private copying, governed by principles of balance, fairness and proportionality. The CPI was also reformed in two ways: it was strengthened in terms of arbitration functions and powers to set substitutory fees and it was empowered to control illegal Internet downloads.

These changes were made in a hasty and non-reflective manner that merely served to highlight the great gap existing between social realities and legislation. Also evident was the government's general indifference to the conflict between public and private interests. Several court judgments and some regulatory reform efforts gradually rectified certain basic aspects of the legal regime, summarized below:

1. Fair compensation for private copying may not be applied indiscriminately without taking into account the use made of the supporting device. If it can be proved that the device for which the levy is paid is not used to copy protected works, then the collection of a fee is not justified. In other words, the indiscriminate application of a private copying levy, in particular, on recording equipment, digital devices and support media clearly reserved for uses other than private copying, is a contravention of Directive 2001/29/EC. Automatically assuming that devices and support media will be used for private copying — an issue which is particularly important in the case of large institutional consumers — is therefore not justified.

2. The Supreme Court has established case law in relation to the calculation of fair compensation for private copying and has imposed a veto on automatic calculations based on turnover. Fair compensation

should be determined on the basis of general fees, as notified by collecting societies to the public administration, and their fair weighting according to the income of the user, taking into account actual use, financial volume of operations and the existence of agreements with other companies performing similar activities.

3. The compensation as established by Article 140 of the LPI for unauthorized photocopying in establishments open to the public — in accordance with the general fees of CEDRO (as the claimant) and the remuneration that would have been received had the photocopying been authorized — is the amount of the general fee for authorized photocopying of 10% of the work, multiplied by five. If evidence clearly indicates that the average percentage photocopied is less or more than 50% of the work, the rate may be multiplied by a higher or lower coefficient, to a maximum of ten times the amount.

4. The amount and method of collection of the digital copying levy, as normatively established by Order PRE/1743/2008, were declared in contravention of the law given that essential requirements regarding approval were not fulfilled, namely, inclusion of the State Council Opinion and the economic dossiers. Its abrogation means that, although amounts paid between 2008 and 2011 cannot be recovered, any collection of the levy was impossible until some similar provision was approved. The reform undertaken by Royal Decree Law 20/2011 cancelled the digital copying levy in favour of publicly funded compensation via a budgetary allocation from the General State Budget. This change is an implicit recognition of the public nature of fair compensation.

5. The CPI was adapted to the new provisions of the LES (Final Provision 43. i.e., the Sinde Law), with resulting changes in its role, in fee-setting (Section I) and in procedures for safeguarding IP rights (Section II). The CPI, further strengthened by Law 21/2104, may now act on its own initiative regarding possible infringements and may

formally request Internet service suspension, the withdrawal of advertising from websites and the blocking of electronic payments.

6. The CPI is no longer merely an arbitrator but an administrative body with powers to set fees. Consequently, its fee-setting and fair compensation functions are recognized as matters of public interest. The choice of an administrative and not a judicial body is legitimate as long as the possibility of court review of the corresponding decisions is guaranteed. The scope of administrative measures for service suspension and content removal, however, may overlap with protective measures in civil law (injunctions).

7. The CPI needs to be provided with the human and financial means necessary for it to exercise the key role it is designed to play in the IP system. It also requires a system of appointments that guarantees both professionalism and independence. Otherwise, despite progress in terms of recognition of the public nature of fair compensation and the greater implication of government, it will be impossible for the CPI to ensure compliance with regulations and to implement the oversight functions entrusted to it.

Acknowledgments

This research has been possible thanks to funding from the Centre d'Estudis i de Recerca d'Humanitats (CERHUM) at the Universitat Autònoma de Barcelona, the European Union ERDF Programme and the Spanish Ministry of Education and Science (Research Project ECO2011-29558-C02-01-E) and the Catalan Autonomous Government/Agència de Gestió d'Ajuts Universitaris i de Recerca (AGAUR) (Grant 2014-SGR-502).

References

Delgado-Porras, A. (1995). Comentarios a la Ley de Propiedad Intelectual. In Albaladejo, M., & Díaz-Alabart, S. (Eds.). *Comentarios al Código Civil y Compilaciones Forales,* V, Vol. 4B. Madrid: Editorial Revista de Derecho Privado-EDERSA. 1006.

Garrote, I. (2006). La copia privada y la compensación por copia privada. In Bercovitz-Rodriguez-Cano, R. (Ed.). *Las Reformas de la Ley de Propiedad Intelectual.* Valencia: Tirant Lo Blanch.

Garrote, I. (2007). Comentario al artículo 25. Compensación equitativa por copia privada. In Bercovitz-Rodriguez-Cano, R. (Ed.). *Comentarios a la Ley de Propiedad Intelectual.* Madrid: Tecnos.

Padros-Reig, C., & López-Sintas, J. (2011). *El canon digital a debate. Revolución tecnológica y consumo cultural en un nuevo marco jurídico-económico.* Barcelona: Atelier.

Perez De Ontiveros-Baquero, C. (1993). 19 de julio de 1993. Propiedad intelectual. Facultad patrimonial de comunicación pública Actos de comunicación pública. Necesidad de autorización del autor, *Cuadernos Civitas de Jurisprudencia Civil*, 33, 953-962.

Rodríguez-Portugués, M. (2013). Reserva de jurisdicción, potestad reglamentaria y propiedad intelectual. En torno a las sentencias del Tribunal Supremo de 31 de mayo de 2013 sobre la denominada Ley Sinde, *Revista de Administración Pública*, 192, 231-256.

Rodríguez-Tapia, J.M. (2007). *Comentarios a la Ley de Propiedad Intelectual.* Madrid: Thomson Civitas.

Seisdedos, I., & Fraguas, A. (2011). La 'ley Sinde' ve la luz con el PP, 30 December, *El País*.
http://cultura.elpais.com/cultura/2011/12/30/actualidad/1325199603_850215.html

Chapter 4

The social construction of music markets: Copyright and technology in the digital age[*]

Jordi López-Sintas[1], Ercilia García-Álvarez[2], Sheila Sánchez-Bergara[2]

[1]Universitat Autònoma de Barcelona, Spain.
[2]Universitat Rovira i Virgili, Spain.
jordi.lopez@uab.es, mariaercilia.garcia@urv.cat, sheila.sanchez@urv.cat

Doi: http://dx.doi.org/10.3926/oms.301

How to cite this chapter

López-Sintas, J., García-Álvarez, E., & Sánchez-Bergara, S. (2015). The social construction of music markets: Copyright and technology in the digital age. In López-Sintas, J. (Ed.). *The social construction of culture markets: Between incentives to creation and access to culture.* Barcelona, Spain: OmniaScience. pp. 101-121.

---

[*] This chapter is based on a presentation given at the 5th Vienna Music Business Research Days, 1-3 October 2014.

J. López-Sintas, E. García-Álvarez, S. Sánchez-Bergara

Abstract

Just as vinyl records transformed local into national music markets several decades ago, digital technologies and the Internet have recently constructed a new kind of popular music market. Given that the existing legal frameworks impeded this transformation, new legislation was required to accommodate new music consumption patterns and new distributions channels. Peterson's production of culture framework suggests that popular music markets are being transformed in terms of legislation, technology, industry structure, organizational structure, market demand and occupational careers. Yet it is legislation regarding copyright and related rights that is the key element in limiting or fostering the construction of a new kind of technology-based popular music market. We analyse the role played by legislation and technology in socially constructed music markets and show how these have transformed the music market in the digital age.

Keywords
Music industries, social construction, copyright, digital age.

1. Introduction

In the early 1970s sociologists proposed studying cultural expressions, not as symbolic systems, but as the product of the social contexts in which they were developed (Hirsch, 1972; DiMaggio & Hirsch, 1976; Peterson & Berger, 1971, 1975). In other words, they proposed applying sociology of knowledge methods to the study of the conditions that gave rise to cultural expressions, as opposed to studying the meaning of symbolic objects as represented by the set of values, norms and beliefs shared by their producers.

Early studies of this paradigm, which Peterson (1976) labelled the "production of culture", focused on the social conditions that gave rise to innovation in music creation. In particular, the diversity of musical genres marketed in the 1960s and early 1970s was studied by Hirsch (1971, 1972) and Peterson and Berger (1971, 1975) using tools developed to study the structure of organizations and industries.

This novel perspective on the production of culture departed from the idea that the symbolic content of cultural expressions depends on the social, legal and economic contexts in which these expressions are created, edited, produced, marketed, purchased and evaluated. Even though this approach may have relied on the analytical tools of organizations and industry, the ultimate goal was to describe the social context in which cultural expressions are created, produced and marketed. In the mid-1980s Peterson (1985) proposed that the social conditions of cultural production could be described according to six distinct facets: (1) technology; (2) legislation; (3) industry structure; (4) organizational structure; (5) the market (in the demand sense); and (6) occupational careers (of artists and technical experts). These six facets constitute a set of institutional and organizational constraints that describe and explain, for instance, the emergence of new music genres or the relationship between market concentration and musical diversity. Peterson (1990) subsequently used this analytical scheme to explain the emergence of rock and roll in 1955.

The production of culture along with the economic, organizational and creative forces that drive the production of cultural expressions determine new technological uses in the same way that new technologies shape cultural objects. Peterson and Anand (2004) have acknowledged that "changes in communication technology profoundly destabilize and create new opportunities in art and culture" (2004: page 314). Nonetheless, although the new technologies may offer new creative possibilities, it is the social context that determines how cultural industries change (Klinenberg & Benzecry, 2005). We show how technological innovation only gives rise to new expressive possibilities when legislation builds the legal object that it aims to regulate (Kretschmer & Pratt, 2009).

Below we describe the different popular music market models that have developed since the invention of sound recording. We do so in a manner similar to White and White (1993), who described how the academy system evolved into the dealer-critic system in the art world. In particular, we demonstrate how legal regulation created markets while also creating the objects to be traded in those markets. Our goal is to contribute to the literature on the social construction of music markets by highlighting how technology and legislation governing copyright and market regulation play a role in constructing music markets in the digital age. In order to demonstrate how music markets are built by the interaction between legislation, technology and stakeholders, we adopted the constructionist perspective of Latour and Woolgar (1986), Latour (2002) and Callon and Law (1982).

Our research is based on data drawn from a number of sources. We first mined the literature for previous research — especially studies that adopted a production of culture perspective (Peterson, 1976, 1985, 1990; Peterson & Anand, 2004) — in order to document the social construction of music markets from the invention of analogue records to date. We also collected and analysed recent music industry reports and statistics. Finally, we analysed the most important technological advances and copyright and related rights legislation in the USA and Europe (mainly) with a view to describing their role in constructing modern-day music markets.

2. From Local Popular Music Markets to Regional Commercial Markets (Circa 1900 to 1939)

Before the invention of the gramophone, popular music was performed in local markets in what could be called a community model of production, with local artists versioning the most popular songs of the day. There were few concerns about copyright, as little economic damage could be wrought in the local markets of other artists from whom one versioned the song. With the advent of the gramophone and recordings of musical productions on flat discs, local markets were transformed into regional commercial markets, giving rise to what Peterson and DiMaggio (1975: page 497) called "emerging culture classes". Cultural differences based on ethnic, regional and socioeconomic class were thus removed, as documented by Peterson and DiMaggio (1975: page 497) for the country music genre. This fact laid the groundwork for the hypothesis of omnivorous musical preferences (Peterson, 2005).

Before the arrival of the gramophone and flat discs, the impact of artists was geographically and physically limited, and, consequently, the market was mainly populated by artists generally known only locally. Gramophone records removed this physical and local constraint, resulting in some performers becoming known outside their local markets. Record labels soon realized, however, that if they held the copyright for any hit song that they recorded and distributed, they could prevent others from recording new versions that would cannibalize their sales.

The invention of gramophones and flat discs along with changes in the regulation of sound recording copyright thus changed the course of popular music markets. In the USA in 1909, paradoxically, opposition by successful performers and composers/lyricists to recorded discs led Congress to review the Copyright Act of 1790 and introduce a 50-cent fee for mechanical reproduction (Tschmuck, 2009; House Report One on the Copyright Act of 1909[1]). This change in copyright law laid the groundwork for the creation, in 1914, of the American Society of Composers, Authors and Publishers (ASCAP), as an organization to license music to radio stations, collect fees

---

1 Available at: http://copyright.gov/history/1909act.pdf

and redistribute revenues to members. From this point on, the interests of sheet music publishers and record labels merged. Another change that completed the social construction of the popular commercial music market was that record labels would only produced records for musicians and performers whose rights they held (Peterson, 1990). Thus, in this market model, the roles of composer/lyricist and performer were separated.

Major labels associated with ASCAP could control regional music markets through ASCAP by exercising a monopoly over both production and promotion and by building a distribution and retailing network that enabled them to decide which music consumers could buy. On the production side, ASCAP members could decide which recordings merited protection under the umbrella of the Copyright Act of 1909. ASCAP could thus control the transformation of a musical creation into a commodity, that is, a private commercial object that could be traded by record labels and then sold to consumers in a monopoly setup. On the promotion side, radio stations were obliged to negotiate rights to broadcast both live performances and reproductions with ASCAP, which meant that only productions registered with ASCAP could be played on air.

Record labels, as well as controlling radio in this regional market model, also enjoyed a high level of control over distribution and retail sales. Although the flat shellac discs used for gramophone recordings were less costly than phonograph cylinders, they were fragile, which meant that they were expensive to distribute. Hence, only the major labels (Warner, EMI, Decca and Polygram) were able to finance — and so control — the means of distribution; they eventually set up their own retail chains to sell music discs to the end consumer (Peterson, 1990).

3. The Construction of National Markets (Circa 1939 to 1980)

A new transformation of the music markets was launched in 1939. The pressure exerted by ASCAP on national radio stations led CBS to buy Columbia Records in 1938. Nonetheless, this kind of vertical integration was affected by new technologies and by regulatory changes — governing both radio and the new TV media and also copyright over new music genres — that played a major role in shaping a different kind of market.

Record labels initially distrusted radio stations — just as the successful composers and performers of the early 1900s had distrusted recorded music and record labels. Their fears for their record sale revenues, as protected by ASCAP, led record labels to impose broadcast fees that radio stations considered intolerable. In 1939 a dispute arose between ASCAP and the National Association of Radio Broadcasters (NARB, now called the National Association of Broadcasters, NAB) as a result of a substantial increase in licensing fees announced by ASCAP. This conflict led to the creation, in 1939, of Broadcast Music Inc (BMI) by the NARB, as a lower-cost alternative source of licensing for music users, including radio stations. To compete with ASCAP, BMI had to first record and then protect new musical creations. It thus enthusiastically welcomed songwriters and publishers from niche musical genres — like jazz, country, Latin, hillbilly, rhythm and blues, and later rock and roll — that tended to be ignored by ASCAP (Hirsch, 1971: page 383). These products were thus turned into commercial commodities that generated copyright revenues from airplay by radio stations and from the sale of records promoted by the same radio stations.

TV, as yet another new medium, brought about further changes in the music industry. Historical evidence shows that TV broadcasting regulation mimicked early radio broadcasting regulation, with almost identical stakeholders. By 1946 the large federal radio stations, CBS, RCA, etc, had entered the TV sector, bringing with them their technical and organizational expertise. A new legislative change liberalized the radio licence market, leading to an increase in the number of radio stations. The impact of BMI combined with this explosion in radio broadcasters resulted in the creation of a new national market. Thanks to the popularity of TV and to BMI's achievement in reducing the cost of recorded music, radio station programming underwent a radical change. From the 1950s the network model started to be replaced by a music radio format based on the "top 40" popular music hits for specific genres, which, in turn, led to the rise of the disc jockey (DJ). Radio, by this stage, was ready to become the main launching pad for the phenomenally successful new genre of rock and roll (Peterson, 1990).

The construction of a national market was further facilitated in 1948 by innovation from Columbia Records in the form of the long playing (LP) 33 ⅓ rpm microgroove vinyl record. This invention enabled recording duration to be lengthened from the 5 minutes of the 78 rpm shellac to more than 20 minutes on each side of the vinyl LP. The LP also led to a reduction in delivery costs as the vinyl record was more robust than the shellac disc. This robustness of the vinyl record also facilitated the entry of independent distributors who supplied new musical genres to independent retailers. Independent distribution and retailing was further aided by the invention of the smaller 45 rpm vinyl record by RCA in 1949. The diffusion of new musical genres, like country music and rock and roll, was thus facilitated by a succession of developments, described in detail by Peterson in his book *Creating Country Music: Fabricating Authenticity* (1997) and in his suggestive article on rock and roll *Why 1955?* (1990).

Musical innovation was featured by a developing relationship between market concentration and musical diversity. According to Peterson and Berger (1975), the concentration of market share among four or eight major labels led to a reduction in the variety of music in the top 40 lists. Lopes (1992) reanalysed this hypothesis, finding that the regularity encountered by Peterson and Berger (1975) was the outcome of the production, promotion and distribution systems used by the major labels.

With the liberalization of radio, promotion strategies changed, with live performances giving way to music programmes and DJs acting as gatekeepers of popular music trends. DJs became so powerful, in fact, that they could bring fame to a musical group overnight (Peterson, 1990). Although the system required the media to be independent, the majors tried to influence music programming by presenting DJs with the music that they wanted to promote and even bribing them to give air time to specific songs. Influencing consumer tastes became vital to controlling the market. The major labels tended to favour concentrating their promotional efforts on a small set of productions and so needed to make decisions early on about which productions to favour. Their interest in influencing the media was therefore aimed at ensuring that their decisions would be profitable.

The importance of DJs as market gatekeepers was further enhanced when new formats facilitated the private recording of music programmes. By the early 1970s most households had good quality cassette players that made acceptable hi-fi recordings. The introduction of portable cassette players (like the Sony Walkman) in the late 1970s and the inclusion of radio-cassette players in cars led to the cassette tape becoming the most popular format by the mid-1980s, even for pre-recorded music. Record labels again reacted to this new invention and, just as CBS — a broadcasting company — had acquired Columbia Records in 1938, so too did Sony — a technology company — take over CBS Records in 1987, renaming the new group Sony Music Entertainment in 1991.

4. The Construction of Transnational Markets (Circa 1980 to 2000)

Philips and Sony independently invented the compact disc (CD) and collaborated to produce a standard recording and playback format — made commercially available from 1982 — that ultimately led to the digitization of music and launched the construction of a transnational market model. Initially Polydor Pressing Operations in Germany and a Japan-based plant supplied the world market for blank CDs. The first popular music CD produced by Philips was Abba's *The Visitors* in 1981; Sony, meanwhile, began marketing the new format with its release of 16 new titles through CBS Records in North America. In 1985, Dire Straits' *Brothers in Arms* album broke the record of one million CD sales and David Bowie became the first artist to have their entire music catalogue recorded on CD. Newer formats like DVD and Blu-ray, even though they improved the technology, did not usher in major changes. By the early 2000s the CD had replaced the radio-cassette player as standard equipment in new cars.

The digitization of music led to a new market configuration, which — following the designation of transnational corporations proposed by Burnett (1990) — we will refer to as the transnational market. This transnational model consisted of three types of operators: transnational corporations, independent majors and indies (smaller, independent labels).

Holding predominant market shares and producing and distributing their own productions were transnational corporations like CBS, EMI, RCA, Warner and Polygram, which, in 1987, represented 84% and 81% of the LP and singles markets, respectively. The traditional majors were now worldwide entertainment conglomerates and, in the 1980s, they adopted what Lopes (1992) termed an "open system of production", which facilitated the incorporation of musical innovation and diversity as a strategy to control the market. The majors started out by buying up specialist jazz, country, rhythm and blues and rock and roll labels and by negotiating distribution agreements with other record labels, to later branch out into other entertainment and leisure markets (as happened with Warner Brothers, which started out in music and then entered film).

Transnational corporations constructed transnational markets through vertical semi-integration and, with the help of the open system of production (Lopes, 1992), exercised control through artist recruitment and distribution agreements signed with the new independent majors and indie record labels. These corporations also controlled recording studios, disc-copying and packaging technologies as well as international marketing, promotion and distribution networks (Burnett, 1990). This US industry model of transnational entertainment company now dominates international markets.

The second type of operator was the independent major — typically an innovative company with independent recording studios, copiers and distributors — that entered the market through distribution agreements with transnational corporations. One such example is Virgin, which has further diversified into film, video and passenger transport. Finally, indie labels — often founded by independent recording studios that decided to form their own labels — operated with other independent operators in the production and distribution chain.

Profitable distribution and promotion by transnational corporations in international markets required, however, that the nations that made up the international market regulate musical productions to protect corporate interests. Hence, negotiations under the auspices of the World Trade Organization (WTO) eventually led to a 1994 agreement encapsulated in a document called Trade-Related Aspects of Intellectual Property Rights (TRIPS), raised as a transnational legal instrument that would protect, beyond national borders, the rights of intellectual property owners (mainly transnational corporations from developed countries).

Enacted two years later — in the framework of the World Intellectual Property Organization (WIPO) — were what came to be known as the "Internet treaties", aimed at adapting copyright and related rights to the digital era: the WIPO Copyright Treaty (WCT) and the WIPO Performances and Phonograms Treaty (WPPT). This reconfiguration of the global legal system governing intellectual property in defence of the interests of the most powerful industries (Drahos, 2004: page 335) was the outcome of intense lobbying by international corporations.

The EU not only adhered to the WIPO Internet treaties; to ensure that the single market was not fragmented by different levels of protection (Larsson, 2011), it enacted Directive 2001/29/EC of the European Parliament and of the Council of 22 May 2001 on the harmonization of certain aspects of copyright and related rights in the information society. This directive was part of a package of measures aimed at establishing a coherent pan-European legal framework that would protect intellectual property rights. In the interest of fostering e-commerce, it horizontally aligned rights while setting aside sectorial harmonization previously performed for computer software, databases and broadcasting via cable or satellite. The directive adapted EU law to the digital environment with such precision that it has left little room for member states to legislate in accordance with their own existing legislation and culture. Consequently, it has been considered to be more of a binding regulation than a mere standard (Garrote, 2001).

The EU took the view of defining property rights broadly and of accommodating different interests by way of exceptions (Garrote, 2001). However, a new right was created for authors, which was the right to authorize making available on-demand services for interactive transmissions to the public; also maintained was the traditional broadcasting services right of public communication. The EU also increased the number of actions that could be criminalized, thereby expanding and strengthening copyright and related rights in Europe (Larsson, 2011).

5. The Construction of Global Markets (Circa 2000 to Date)

The transformation of musical productions into intangible products was the result of two technological advances: (1) the invention of the MP3 (MPEG audio layer III) compression format; and (2) the development of Internet services for sharing compressed files. Other proprietary formats exist that allow music file-sharing (e.g., AAC, ALAC and AIFF, used by Apple for iTunes downloads, and WAV and WMA, developed by Microsoft) but these have not disrupted music market functioning because they are used in digital distribution channels that mimic traditional channels.

The combination of the MP3 format and new Internet services has meant that music has recovered the public good property it had in the local popular music markets of the beginning of the 20th century, notwithstanding copyright law provisions (Hougaard & Tvede, 2010). These technological advances have meant that musical productions could be digitized and compressed with hardly any quality loss for online distribution beyond the control of record labels. They consequently laid the foundations for the transformation of the structure, organization and legal system underpinning transnational markets.

The record labels (along with other entertainment sectors) reacted by manifesting their opposition to these developments, which were undermining their business model based on material sales and control over promotion and distribution. They took their fight to the international stage, exerting pressure on national governments to expand copyright and related rights and to limit exceptions (which, by affecting technological tools, contravened the laws of a number of countries, including Spain). This response is hardly a novel one, as the historical evidence shows that copyright and related rights legislation has invariably been characterized by the protection of traditional monopolies against changes in reproduction and communication media (Frith, 1988). This is why Frith (1988) suggests that copyright is no longer merely a question of morals but is also a political and economic issue.

Digitized music and the Internet have opened up new ways of promoting musical productions. Competing with radio and television stations operated by major corporations — often controlled by transnational corporations — are new socially organized media such as file-sharing networks and social media like YouTube. The important qualitative difference between promoting musical creations through the traditional media and through the new online social media is that music promotion is no longer monopolized by music transnationals, with the outcome that the market is coming to be populated by new artists, consumers and economic stakeholders.

The new media have a transcendence that goes beyond the size of the markets, as they imply a radical change in sources of income for artists and record labels. Whereas live concerts and traditional media were typically used to promote selected artists (Hirsch, 1972), nowadays anyone can use the social media to promote their musical creations and so attract followers and create a fan base. Furthermore, the fact that demand for live music concerts has grown — along with the cost of tickets — since the beginning of the 21st century has benefited creators and performers with little exposure to traditional media, not to mention web-based technology businesses.

The strong opposition of the record labels — whether transnational corporations, new majors or even indies — to the online sharing of musical productions was only to be expected. The transnational corporations' response was to focus on harmonizing mechanisms to protect their economic interests. The EU responded by enacting Directive 2004/48/EC of the European Parliament and of the Council of 29 April 2004 on the enforcement of intellectual property rights, which seeks to guarantee monopolies in cultural productions by harmonizing legislation on implementing measures in order, in turn, to harmonize the enforcement of intellectual property rights in the internal market. However, although the initial Commission proposal contained measures aimed at harmonizing penalty proceedings, the directive as finally adopted only included provisions to regulate civil proceedings (Berenguer, 2004). In addition, the final version of the directive provides that states may adopt measures other than those specified. Berenguer (2004) argues, consequently, that the fact that only civil proceedings and not penalty proceedings have been harmonized is evidence of the presence of new economic interests in EU negotiation procedures.

As for artist revenues, the record labels have retaken control over these via the new 360-degree deals ("multiple rights deal", according to record company representatives). With these agreements, record labels derive revenues from all possible income sources of artists, thereby making up for the reduction in income from CD sales and taking advantage of the growth in demand for live concerts (Marshall, 2013). Thus, in return for record label support in marketing and promoting their musical productions, artists agree to give the record label a percentage of all their income, irrespective of whether it comes from album sales, live concerts, movies, fan clubs, merchandise or any other source.

Technological advances and demand for digital music have created the conditions for the development of other approaches to distribution and sale. One example is the digital variant on traditional distribution channels, as represented by Apple's iTunes store and Amazon. Whereas Apple transforms musical productions into intangible products that are rematerialized via the iPod, Amazon combines the analogue and digital concepts by simultaneously selling its customers physical disks and a digital version. Although this business model may seem to represent yet another channel, the difficulties experienced by both Apple and Amazon in negotiating distribution agreements with music transnationals would suggest otherwise. Unlike traditional outlets, which merely had access to information on demand and its geographical distribution, digital distribution channels collect detailed information on what people are listening to, listener profiles, trends, etc.

Another very different business model is music streaming, represented by companies such as Spotify, Deezer and Musicover, and based on the creation of their own rights management societies. Since the sheer numbers of musical productions is such that the cost of contacting all owners of copyright and related rights would be impractical, these services rely on content aggregators to negotiate streaming rights with artists and record labels. Copyright fees are paid to authors according to the number of times a musical production has been streamed by clients. A streaming service, which is like radio on demand, is typically offered in the form of free and paid options. Free streaming usually aims to promote musical productions and, as with traditional radios, the source of income is advertising. Paid streaming typically gives access to a larger catalogue of recordings, allows unlimited reproduction and offers additional services such as the exclusion of advertisements, higher quality audio, etc.

Given the ubiquity of the digital environment it was evident that users of music for commercial purposes needed a policy on licensing. As new stakeholders have acquired economic importance, they have become increasingly vociferous in their demand for an advantageous regulatory environment for their companies. At the EU level, a regulatory framework is gradually being built that, by granting legal protection to the opportunities offered by the digital technologies, favours the development of new business models.

The lack of a single EU-wide licence or equivalent mechanism initially posed a major obstacle to business expansion into new territories and the enlargement of music catalogues. Some ten years ago, a study by the Commission of the European Communities (2005) highlighted the need to reconsider cross-border management of online music copyright and related rights. It proposed — in response to a demand from commercial users of the new digital music services, who had to negotiate in different conditions from country to country — that right holders should be able to freely choose their rights manager for the entire EU.

Commission Recommendation 2005/737/EC of 18 May 2005 on collective cross-border management of copyright and related rights for legitimate online music services was a first step towards improving licensing at the EU level so as to include new webcasting, streaming and on-demand download services. This recommendation, even with its inherent limitations, has therefore established more favourable conditions for online music service providers.

More recently, the EU enacted Directive 2014/26/EU of the European Parliament and of the Council of 26 February 2014 on collective management of copyright and related rights and multi-territorial licensing of rights in musical works for online use in the internal market. This minimum harmonization directive provides for transposition into national legislation by 10 April 2016. Its guiding principles are the right holders' freedom to choose their rights manager and to withdraw authorization by giving a maximum of six months' notice. Regarding multi-territorial licenses for online musical production rights, rights managers are required to be able to accurately and transparently determine which works and which rights belong to their catalogues. They are also required to be accurate and timely in invoicing and delivery. This new model of collective rights management prevents monopolies and promotes competition by facilitating new entrants.

The digital technologies have transformed the global monopolies held by the major labels over the production, promotion and distribution of musical productions. Thus, currently coexisting along with the CD are multiple products and services designed to meet all market segment needs (Waelbrock,

2013). To brick-and-mortar stores we can now add online stores, music streaming and cloud storage services. New Internet spaces in which to connect with the public coexist and develop alongside traditional promotional channels. Laws on copyright and related rights have helped to create a new model of collective rights management at the EU level that has undone the monopolies of the collecting societies, enhanced competition and opened up new business opportunities.

6. Discussion and Conclusions

The above description of the construction of local, regional, national, transnational and global markets demonstrates how technological advances have opened up new creative and business opportunities that only materialize once suitable legislation is in place. Although technological advances have launched a series of different transformations of the music market, it is legal regulation which, in fact, has allowed transformations to happen. In all the cases described, dominant market stakeholders launched processes to ensure legal protection against new technological developments and product innovations. Their interest has always been to keep firm control of the music markets in order to limit the repercussions of the new technologies on their privileged revenue flows. This was also the reason behind the modification of US copyright law back in 1909, demanded by popular artists of the day, who failed to see the transformation that was underway in their markets.

The ability to fix sound recordings on a suitable support reduced the physical limitations of local markets, allowed the emergence of new stakeholders in the form of record labels and transformed music into a commodity that could be traded in the marketplace. This process facilitated the construction of the first commercial markets at the regional level, based on the new record labels taking control of musical productions from artists. Something similar happened once technological advances perfected hardware and made music broadcasts possible through radio and later TV.

TV, in fact, played a major, if indirect, transformative role. Radio stations expanded into the TV sector, bringing with them their creative and technical expertise, at a time when the radio market was liberalized. The media, by becoming the main instruments for the promotion of new commercial musical genres, thus built a national market.

With the digitization of music, markets again changed course, with control over promotion and distribution in transnational markets enhanced by the CD, which offered better quality and greater capacity. However, digitization required legislative changes to international trade agreements. Thus, multinational corporations lobbied their governments — first under the WTO and then under the WIPO — to sign agreements that ensured the protection of their rights. These agreements would facilitate the construction of transnational markets.

However, further advances in digital technologies (MP3 and file-sharing networks) subverted the transnational business model based on material musical productions. Further legislative changes were necessary, so — again under the umbrella of the WTO and WIPO — transnational corporations influenced law-making at the national level (as is widely documented for countries like Spain, France and Brazil). They also lobbied their own governments to extend copyright terms.

Transnational corporations have also resisted the dematerialization of digital music production. In focusing on the promotion, distribution and sale of material productions, they lost out on the technological innovations that characterized the early 21st century. It is no accident that the CD as a musical support was invented, not by music corporations, but by two consumer electronics corporations: Sony in Japan and Philips in the Netherlands. In the construction of transnational music markets, therefore, technological innovation took place in the consumer electronics sector. Eventually, however, as had happened in the early 20th century, technological innovators entered the music market.

Global markets needed to be able to compress music productions to facilitate their circulation over the Internet. This technology was held, however, by companies such as Apple, Amazon and Google. Rather unwillingly, record labels finally signed agreements with these companies to distribute their music catalogues, but at a high price: (1) they have ceded control over distribution to new online music providers and intermediaries; and (2) they have ceded control over promotion to the new social media.

In conclusion, both laws and cultural expressions reflect and define the values and interests of a society. Changes to copyright and related rights legislation, however, over and above any consideration of actual rights, have also reflected pragmatic decisions about who should benefit and how from musical productions (Frith, 1988). In the construction of music markets, the major industry stakeholders have secured control over production, promotion, distribution and access to musical productions by redefining, for each advance of the technological frontier, what should be protected, how and for how long. Therefore, although technological advances have configured transformations of the music market, it is copyright laws which have ultimately enabled the transformations to take place.

Acknowledgments

This research has been possible thanks to funding from the Centre d'Estudis i de Recerca d'Humanitats (CERHUM) at the Universitat Autònoma de Barcelona, the European Union ERDF Programme and the Spanish Ministry of Education and Science (Research Project ECO2011-29558-C02-01-E) and the Catalan Autonomous Government/Agència de Gestió d'Ajuts Universitaris i de Recerca (AGAUR) (Grant 2014-SGR-502).

References

Berenguer, F. (2004). Análisis crítico de la Directiva 2004/48/CE relativa al respeto de los Derechos de Propiedad Intelectual. *Gaceta Jurídica de la Unión Europea y de la Competencia*, 231, May/June. Madrid: EINSA. 12-28.

Burnett, R. (1990). *Concentration and diversity in the international phonogram industry*. PhD Dissertation. Gothenburg: University of Gothenburg.

Callon, M., & Law, J. (1982). On Interests and their Transformation: Enrolment and Counter-Enrolment. *Social Studies of Science*, 12(4), 615-625.
http://dx.doi.org/10.1177/030631282012004006

Commission of the European Communities (2005). *Study on a community initiative on the cross-border collective management of copyright.* Commission Staff Working Document. Brussels.
http://ec.europa.eu/internal_market/copyright/docs/management/study-collectivemgmt_en.pdf

DiMaggio, P., & Hirsch, P.M. (1976). Production Organizations in the Arts. *American Behavioral Scientist*, 19(6), 735-752.
http://dx.doi.org/10.1177/000276427601900605

Drahos, P. (2004). The regulation of public goods. *Journal of International Economic Law*, 7(2), 321-339.
http://dx.doi.org/10.1093/jiel/7.2.321

Frith, S. (1988). Copyright and the Music Business. *Popular Music*, 7(1), 57–75.
http://dx.doi.org/10.1017/S0261143000002531

Garrote, I. (2001). *El derecho de autor en Internet. La directiva sobre derechos de autor y derechos afines en la sociedad de la información*. Granada: Editorial Comares.

Hirsch, P.M. (1971). Sociological approaches to the pop music phenomenon. *American Behavioral Scientist*, 14(3), 371-388.
http://dx.doi.org/10.1177/000276427101400310

Hirsch, P. (1972). Processing fads and fashions: An organization-set analysis of cultural industry systems. *American Journal of Sociology*, 77(4), 639-659.
http://dx.doi.org/10.1086/225192

Hougaard, J.L., & Tvede, M. (2010). Selling digital music: business models for public goods. *NETNOMICS: Economic Research and Electronic Networking*, 11(1), 85-102.
http://dx.doi.org/10.1007/s11066-009-9047-0

Klinenberg, E., & Benzecry, C. (2005). Introduction: Cultural Production in a Digital Age. *Annals of the American Academy of Political and Social Science*, 597, 6-18.
http://dx.doi.org/10.1177/0002716204270420

Kretschmer, M., & Pratt, A.C. (2009). Legal Form and Cultural Symbol. *Information, Communication and Society*, 12(2), 165-177.
http://dx.doi.org/10.1080/13691180802459930

Larsson, S. (2011). *Metaphors and Norms. Understanding Copyright Law in a Digital Society*. Lund: Media-Tryck.

Latour, B., & Woolgar, S. (1986). *Laboratory Life: The Construction of Scientific Facts*. Princeton: Princeton University Press.

Latour, B. (2002). *La Fabrique du droit: une ethnographie du Conseil d'État*. Paris: La Découverte.

Lopes, P. (1992). Innovation and diversity in the popular music industry, 1969 to 1990. *American Sociological Review*, 57(1), 56-71.
 http://dx.doi.org/10.2307/2096144

Marshall, L. (2013). The 360 deal and the "new" music industry. *European Journal of Cultural Studies*, 16(1), 77-99.
 http://dx.doi.org/10.1177/1367549412457478

Peterson, R.A. (1976). The Production of Culture. A Prolegomenon. *American Behavioral Scientist*, 19(6), 669-684.
 http://dx.doi.org/10.1177/000276427601900601

Peterson, R.A. (1985). Six constraints on the production of literary works. *Poetics*, 14, 45-67.
 http://dx.doi.org/10.1016/0304-422X(85)90004-X

Peterson, R.A. (1990). Why 1955? Explaining the advent of rock music. *Popular Music*, 9(1), 97-116.
 http://dx.doi.org/10.1017/S0261143000003767

Peterson, R.A. (1997). *Creating Country Music: Fabricating Authenticity*. Chicago, IL: University of Chicago Press.

Peterson, R.A. (2005). Problems in comparative research: The example of omnivorousness. *Poetics*, 33(5-6), 257–282.
 http://doi.org/10.1016/j.poetic.2005.10.002

Peterson, R.A., & Anand, N. (2004). The Production of Culture Perspective. *Annual Review of Sociology*, 30(1), 311-334.
 http://dx.doi.org/10.1146/annurev.soc.30.012703.110557

Peterson, R.A., & DiMaggio P. (1975). From region to class, the changing locus of country music: A test of the massification hypothesis. *Social Forces*, 53(3), 497-506.
 http://dx.doi.org/10.1093/sf/53.3.497

Peterson, R.A., & Berger, D. (1975). Cycles in symbol production: The case of popular music. *American Sociological Review*, 40(2), 158-173.
 http://dx.doi.org/10.2307/2094343

Peterson, R.A., & Berger, D. (1971). Entrepreneurship in organizations: evidence from the popular music industry. *Administrative Science*, 10(1), 97-107.
 http://dx.doi.org/10.2307/2391293

Tschmuck, P. (2009). Copyright, Contracts and Music Production. *Information, Communication and Society*, 12(2), 251-266.
 http://dx.doi.org/10.1080/13691180802459971

Waelbroeck, P. (2013). Digital music. In Towse, R. & Handke, C. (Eds.). *Handbook on the Digital Creative Economy*. Northampton: Edward Elgar. 389-400.
 http://dx.doi.org/10.4337/9781781004876.00047

White, H.C., & White C.A. (1993) *Canvases and Careers: Institutional Changes in the French Painting World*. Chicago: University of Chicago Press.

CHAPTER 5

A contextual theory of accessing music: Consumer behaviour and ethical arguments[*]

Ercilia García-Álvarez[1], Jordi López-Sintas[2], Konstantina Zerva[2]

[1]Universitat Rovira i Virgili de Tarragona, Spain.
[2]Universitat Autònoma de Barcelona, Spain.

mariaercilia.garcia@urv.cat, jordi.lopez@uab.es, konstantina.zerva@udg.edu

Doi: http://dx.doi.org/10.3926/oms.302

How to cite this chapter

García-Álvarez, E., López-Sintas, J., & Zerva, K. (2015). A contextual theory of accessing music: Consumer behaviour and ethical arguments. In López-Sintas, J. (Ed.). *The social construction of culture markets: Between incentives to creation and access to culture.* Barcelona, Spain: OmniaScience. pp. 123-160.

---

[*] This chapter, published in *Consumption Markets and Culture*, Volume 12, Issue 3, 2009, pp. 243-264, is reproduced with kind permission from Taylor Francis.

Abstract

Previous research into the ethics of accessing information goods using alternative means (the informal economy or social exchanges) has failed to study the moral arguments used by music consumers to justify their behaviour or explain actions they considered to be (un)ethical. To fill this gap, we conducted a study from the perspective of music consumers in which we grounded a theory that would explain and predict individual arguments and behaviour. Our findings suggest that the morality of accessing culture depends on the social, economic and cultural context in which an individual has been raised. Interestingly, this contextual aspect interacts with economic and cultural resources, affecting the moral arguments used to justify behaviour. Lastly, we describe a model that explains variations in the contextual theory in regard to accessing music and that predicts consumer behaviour in other countries that can be classified in either of the two contexts delineated in our research.

Keywords

Ethical decision making, music consumption, peer-to-peer networks, consumer research, social exchanges, accessing music, grounded theory.

1. Introduction[1]

The ethics of accessing information goods through alternative means, whether in the informal economy or through social exchanges, has been studied mostly for the field of computer software. Many researchers. assuming that software and music consumption by alternative means is unethical, have attempted to find support for the supposed connection between morality and this kind of consumption behaviour (Cohen & Cornwell, 1989; Coyle, Gould, Gupta & Gupta, 2009; Kuo & Hsu, 2001; Xiaohe, 2006). However, the results seem to have yielded negative or, at best, incomplete answers to the ethics test. Most researchers have adopted a narrow focus, assuming that consumers interpret alternative access to information goods as morally wrong and that behavioural differences are explained by differences in ethical postures. Consequently, much research has been limited to a quantitative representation of ethical decision making (Solomon & O'Brien, 1990; Cohen & Cornwell, 1989; Moore & McMullan, 2004) or to a quest for motives arising in an economic framework (Lau, 2006; Bishop, 2002; Husted, 2000). Previous research has largely been based on nationally and socially homogeneous samples and so has failed to take context into account in studying moral arguments justifying behaviour, actions considered to be (un)ethical and differences between arguments and actions. This situation reveals a clear gap in terms of our understanding of the entire spectrum of consumer moral reasoning and behaviour.

Our aim was to study the different ways in which people obtained access to music (copying music albums from friends, buying unauthorized CDs or downloading music from peer-to-peer (P2P) networks) and the moral arguments used to justify use of these options. We used the grounded theory approach (Glaser & Strauss, 1967) to conceptualize and model the complex social process for accessing and consuming music. This approach is based on building a theory capable of explaining and predicting individual arguments and actions regarding access to symbolic goods — such as musical productions — by alternative means. Grounded theory allows the researcher

---

1 All translations of cited material are by Ailish Maher.

to obtain a wealth of data representing different realities and sources, while focusing on meaning and interpretative understanding (Charmaz, 2000).

Our findings suggest that the morality of people's actions regarding access to culture depends on the social, economic and cultural context in which they operate. Buying CDs in the informal economy was considered morally wrong by people raised in a context with abundant public resources for accessing music, but morally acceptable by people who were not so fortunate. Accessing music through P2P networks was considered acceptable by all the interviewees, however. Social context and economic and cultural personal resources also affected consumer behaviour and moral arguments. In countries with abundant public resources, people justified downloading music by comparing it to borrowing music from a library (just more convenient) or viewed it as a way to avoid being exploited by record labels when they liked only one or a few tracks on a CD album. In contrast, people raised in countries with scarce public resources for accessing music were not troubled by the morality of buying CDs in the informal market or downloading music from P2P networks (if they could afford an Internet connection), because, as our theory suggests, they lacked public alternatives.

Again, the availability of public and personal resources for accessing music divided interviewees when it came to changing their behaviour in response to a hypothetical punishment for using alternative ways to access music. The more fortunate in public resources said they would stop downloading music if financial penalties were high, while the other interviewees said they would continue downloading and buying in the informal economy, given that they had no other public alternatives for accessing music.

Our paper focuses on the fact that actions and ethical arguments used to justify individual behaviours are affected by contextual differences, including personal resources. Thus, an understanding of contextual differences is the key to explaining and predicting consumer decisions. Along this vein, we present a theory that explains possible variations in the contextual theory of accessing music and suggest, furthermore, a way to generalize this theory to other countries when classified as belonging to one of the two contexts delineated above

2. Literature Review

Although music was, in the past, mostly a form of cultural expression, it gradually became merchandise exchanged through market mechanisms controlled by major record firms (Peterson & Berger, 1975; Peterson, 1990, 1997). Songs used to belong to the public domain and any interpreter could make their own version. To transform the pleasures of listening to music into the pleasures of consuming music, it became necessary to establish material rights over this expression of culture (Peterson, 1997).

With music as merchandise, the power of recording firms resided in the dependence of customers wishing to access recorded musical productions (Emerson, 1962). The internationalization of music consumption led record firms to set prices that maximized global income while minimizing transactions in the grey market. Since many consumers felt that the price of music albums was unreasonably high (Lau, 2006), alternative ways to access music emerged: copying the albums of friends, borrowing albums from a public library, buying unauthorized copies of CDs, and, more recently, downloading music from the Internet.

These alternative ways of accessing music arose spontaneously as technology, culture, economy, law and society interacted (Peterson, 1990), but were also encouraged by the tight control exercised by record firms over the music market (Spitz & Hunter, 2005; Lau, 2006). Consequently, interest has arisen in whether conventional or alternative access, use and consumption of information goods are associated with an ethical posture. It has been proposed that people confronted with ethical problems attempt to resolve them by appealing to moral standards and moral reasoning (Lau, 2006). Most research conducted to date assumes that traditional moral values and arguments are universal (Hendry, 2001) — a stance that partially mirrors the interests of record labels in punishing deviant conduct, calling it immoral (Spitz & Hunter, 2005) and demanding legislative change to increase punishment (Bishop, 2002).

2.1. Determinants of Alternative Access to Digital Products

Much research has been conducted into the software industry in order to understand the relationship between ethics and action. However, few studies have been made of music production and consumption. Researchers who use the ethical decision-making framework (Thong & Yap, 1998) have accepted the traditional posture of universal moral arguments and values to interpret access to software products by alternative means as simply wrong and immoral (Hendry, 2001). As a consequence, research has sought to establish an association between a scale of ethics and personal behaviour. Yet this kind of research does not appear to produce the desired results in consumer behaviour (Cohen & Cornwell, 1989; Lau, 2006; Logsdon, Thompson & Reid, 1994; Lee, Eining & Long, 1994; Peace, 1997).

Leaving aside the moral decision-making perspective on copying information goods for personal use, other researchers have attempted to find a more specific connection between motives, norms and copying activity. They found that: (1) there were significant differences in software copying practices depending on gender, age, religious orientation, knowledge of copyright, availability of original software and personal benefits (Simpson, Banerjee & Simpson Jr., 1994; Sims, Cheng & Teegen, 1996; Taylor & Shin, 1993; Oz, 2001; Wagner & Sanders, 2001); (2) copying software was considered to be neither illegal nor unethical (Moore & McMullan, 2004; Cohen & Cornwell, 1989; Solomon & O'Brian, 1990) but there were cultural differences in moral arguments (Swinyard, Rinne & Kau, 1990); (3) individual and peer beliefs regarding copying software — based on social justifications, paradigms and special circumstances — were related to intentions to copy software (Al-Jabri & Abdul-Gader, 1997); and (4) the intention to copy was related to the perceived equity or fairness of relationships or exchanges with others, that is, to the perceived ratio of what was received in relation to what was brought to the exchange (Glass & Wood, 1996).

In the specific context of P2P music sharing, the ethics variable has been introduced in limited cases. For instance, Xiaohe (2006) described the development of P2P file sharing and disputes concerning Chinese copyright laws. This author has suggested that file sharing is not consistent with the ethics of legislation and property law because, in the end, it deprives artists of the right to benefit from their work. Easley (2005) investigated the ethical issues underlying file sharing, concluding that, while the illegal nature of file sharing was clear, what was not so clear was the unethical nature of the practice. This author also questioned the ethical behaviour of music labels suing their customers, controlling music promotion through payola and overpricing music, which, as a consequence of the new technologies, has been transformed into a public good (Easley, 2005).

Nonetheless, in research that has taken P2P user opinions into consideration, the results in regard to ethical issues are not so controversial. Condry (2004) analysed the results of surveys conducted in 2003 and 2004 with students, concluding that although P2P users felt that downloading was illegal, it was justified by their antipathy towards music labels. On a further level, Giesler and Pohlmann (2003) conducted a netnographic analysis of Napster consumption meanings from 40 cyber-interviews, suggesting that P2P users felt that music that was downloaded was not obtained unethically but was, rather, a gift from other peers.

For a sample of high school students, Shang, Chen and Chen (2007) explored the impact of several conflicting norms (anti-piracy, free software ideology, reciprocity, consumer rights and user ethical decisions) on various ways of using the P2P network to share copyrighted music files and also studied the reasons why people used the system in different ways. The study identified consumer rights as the main justification for sharing; however, it excluded the impact of contextual differences, acknowledging that the sharing process was too complex to be analysed by survey research.

2.2. A Critical Assessment of Research Conducted to Date

Researchers have probably been asking the wrong question. Most research conducted to date has attempted to identify a relationship between an ethical scale and self-reported software copying practices (Logsdon et al., 1994; Lee et al., 1994; Peace, 1997). Since this kind of research presupposed that copying software for personal use was wrong, people were not asked whether the action was ethically questionable: if most people do not consider it wrong, then no association between the ethical scale and software or music copying practices will exist, as reported. Some research questioned whether people considered copying software to be socially and ethically acceptable or not, finding it, in the end, acceptable (Cohen & Cornwell, 1989; Solomon & O'Brian, 1990). As far as we are aware, no research has asked what behaviours are considered to be morally right or wrong and why, nor has research assessed how answers to these questions might vary according to context and social status.

Samples lack variety in terms of social context and social status. Most samples were compiled in a single country among professionally homogenous groups; thus, for example, research has been conducted among undergraduate and graduate students in the USA (Cohen & Cornwell, 1989; Coyle et al., 2009; Glass & Wood, 1996; Simpson et al., 1994; Logsdon et al., 1994; Peace, 1997; Wagner & Sander, 2001), among students in China (Lee et al., 1994; Xiaohe, 2006), in Singapore (Thong & Yap, 1998; Swinyard et al., 1990) and Saudi Arabia (Al-Jabri & Abdul-Gader, 1997) and among business executives and university teachers (Taylor & Shim, 1993; Oz, 2001). The lack of contextual variety makes it impossible to determine whether there were cultural differences in perspectives on ethical behaviours, motives and fairness in the exchange between firms and individuals. This kind of research design not only reduced variation in the dependent variable (whether contextual or individual), but also in predictors.

To overcome these drawbacks, we developed a qualitative research design aimed at determining: (1) the means (conventional or alternative) that consumers use to access music; (2) the moral arguments used to justify behaviour; and (3) the circumstances in which individuals would be willing to change their behaviour.

3. Methodology

Research within the framework of ethical decision making has not been able to identify consumer actions considered to be ethical or unethical and the moral arguments used to justify actions. Although other research approaches, such as situational research, equity theory and motivational research, have been more successful in identifying predictors of consumer behaviour, they have been unable to demonstrate differences in means of accessing culture or how consumer behaviour might be inspired by moral judgments that vary according to social status.

The aim of our research was to study people who access music by alternative means and to identify core processes in resolving the moral questions posed by different choices. Our purpose was also to generate concepts and relationships that could interpret, explain, account for and predict: (1) variations in how people access music through alternative means; and (2) variations in how individuals justify their actions (that is, how the principles of right and wrong guided their ethical behaviour).

We sought to analyse the social processes occurring during music consumption, focusing on understanding the complexity of this social phenomenon by listening to, observing and interpreting the actions of people as they accessed music by alternative means. To achieve our goal of producing a theory grounded in the actions and arguments of individuals, we used the grounded theory approach initially proposed by Glaser and Strauss (1967) and further developed by Strauss (1987); we also applied the interpretive framework developed by Charmaz (2000).

Since any attempt to comprehend a social reality must be grounded in a person's experience of that activity (Denzin & Lincoln, 1994), concepts, theories and models are developed from the socially constructed knowledge of participants. This methodology has been found suitable for developing consumer-based theories of experiential consumer behaviour (Goulding, 2000), because it makes it easier to understand similarities and differences in the experiences of people who share the same events or circumstances.

3.1. Data

Sampling. Obtaining alternative access to music (copying music albums from friends, borrowing from libraries, buying unauthorized CDs or downloading music from P2P networks) is a popular practice among young people (Shang et al., 2007). We chose a Spanish university as an appropriate context in which to begin building a heterogeneous sample that would ensure richness of data, with the idea being to understand a comprehensive spectrum of moral reasoning and behaviour for consumers accessing music in alternative ways. Our sampling process began with a criterion-based selection of individuals, then continued with snowball, or chain, sampling (Patton, 2002), whereby key informants were identified after asking the first interviewees about friends who also downloaded music — particularly friends of other ages and nationalities and with different music preferences and economic resources. We thus ensured that our data derived from a heterogeneous sample.

Our final sample consisted of young individuals (aged up to 36) from a number of European and Latin American countries, all resident in Barcelona (Spain), with different social, cultural and economic living conditions (also heterogeneous within each country). Of the 23 individuals in our sample, 14 were from countries with relatively abundant public resources for accessing music (Chile, Greece and Spain) and nine were from countries with scarce public resources for accessing music (Argentina, Brazil, Bulgaria and Mexico).

We conducted personal interviews with these interviewees, who all habitually accessed music by alternative means. As the data-grounded theory developed, negative instances were encountered, indicating that additional interviews were needed (based on theoretical sampling) in order to either: (1) reformulate the theory and accommodate the negative instances; or (2) reduce the explanatory range of the theory and omit deviant observations (Glaser & Strauss, 1967; Strauss, 1987). Table 1 provides a breakdown of the final sample of 23 individuals.

Table 1. Interviewee profiles

Name	Age	Nationality	Cultural capital (education level)	Economic capital
Pau	19	Spanish	Secondary	High
Llomár	25	Brazilian	Undergraduate	High
Andreu	20	Spanish	Secondary	Low
Katerina	24	Greek	Graduate	High
Christos	28	Greek	Undergraduate	Low
Giannis	23	Greek	Graduate	High
Jean	32	Spanish	Secondary	High
Albert	18	Spanish	Secondary	Low
Ana	25	Spanish	Undergraduate	Low
Cayetana	14	Mexican	Secondary	Low
Alexandros	25	Greek	Undergraduate	Low
Jaume	36	Spanish	Undergraduate	Low
Dolores	28	Chilean	Graduate	High
Joan	23	Spanish	Secondary	Low
Elena	27	Bulgarian	Graduate	High
Jorge	29	Chilean	Graduate	Low
Carlos	28	Mexican	Graduate	Low
José	32	Argentinian	Graduate	High
Sara	28	Spanish	Secondary	Low
Marta	26	Mexican	Graduate	High
Judith	30	Mexican	Graduate	Low
Antonio	30	Mexican	Graduate	High
Lorena	28	Mexican	Graduate	High

Fieldwork. All interviews were conducted by the third author at the interviewee's home, office or university (wherever they kept their personal music and computers). The interviewees showed the researcher how they organized their music files and the downloading programs they used. Face-to-face interviews provided experiential narrative material and brought up specific phrases and expressions, subsequently important for interpreting the reasons why these consumers accessed music by alternative means. Researcher access to file structures, content and the personal downloading environment of interviewees helped triangulate information.

Prior to interview, the participants — who were assured of anonymity, informed of the purpose of the research and of their right to stop the interview at any time — gave their consent. The interviews, which lasted between 60 and 90 minutes, were digitally recorded (Sony Hi-MD MZ-NH700) and then transcribed verbatim. Initial interviews were broad-ranging, allowing respondents to express their opinion freely; subsequent interviews were aimed at obtaining more targeted information and so were designed on the basis of concepts generated in the initial interviews and on a search for negative evidences following the paths generated by the constant comparative analysis.

The interviews were conducted using plain everyday language (see Seale, 1999: page 34) and the protocol questions focused on identifying the social processes behind music consumption, including ways of accessing music, arguments used to justify behaviour and interviewee social practices in regard to the enjoyment of music.

3.2. Analysis

Interview transcripts, observation notes and secondary data were imported into MaxQDA 2007, a computer-assisted qualitative data analysis software (CAQDAS). Given the aim of the research, we applied a coding process for hypothesis generation (Kelle & Laurie, 1995). The coding scheme was constructed simultaneously with the ongoing data analysis process in which the analytical framework, categories and properties emerged. Because sampling and coding took place simultaneously in an unstructured setting and with the close involvement of researchers with an intimate knowledge of the field, the codes tended to convey subjective interpretations. In order to control possible sources of coding errors (Tschudi, 1989), the research team was composed of a junior researcher who did the fieldwork, a senior researcher involved in qualitative data analysis and the substantive field and a third analyst from the research methods field who acted as auditor. The different theoretical perspectives and interests of the three researchers aimed to minimize bias in the coding of text passages and obtain a consistent coding schema (Kelle & Laurie, 1995: page 27).

According to the interpretive paradigm, the meaning of human action and interaction can only be adequately understood if the interpretations and common-sense knowledge of actors are taken into account (Wilson, 1970; Giddens, 1976; Denzin, 1989). Consequently, we applied the three principles formulated by Richards and Richards (1995: page 87 and ff) for category structure construction: (1) general to specific, meaning that properties and dimensions should be cases of a general or specific category; (2) consistence, meaning that the description of a given category should apply to all the categories and capture lower-level properties and dimensions; and (3) parsimony, meaning that one topic or idea should occur in only one place in the category system.

In the open-coding phase, we began with a line-by-line microanalysis of all our transcripts and observation data and collected numerous illustrative quotes to saturate categories. We then refined our initial list of categories, made connections between them and defined properties by axial coding. In constructing the category structure, whenever a theoretical insight occurred to us we stopped coding so as to write a memo that we associated with one or more categories (see Glaser & Strauss, 1967: page 107; Glaser 1978: page 83). In fact, the main theoretical ideas emerged as we conducted the open and axial coding phases (Strauss, 1987; Strauss & Corbin, 1991). Finally, in the selective coding phase we identified core categories and themes from which theory would be derived and then integrated the different hypotheses into the theory and refined it. Interviews with other individuals were necessary in order to ensure data redundancy and to locate secondary sources that helped saturate categories and accommodate initially deviant observations into a richer theory.

In constructing the theory, we looked for patterns reflecting alternative ways of accessing music and moral arguments used to justify actions that responded to local context and personal living conditions. Both local contexts and personal capital interacted to offer alternative options that facilitated or hindered access to music and, to some extent, to explain how people accessed music and why. As the category structure was formed, guided by theoretical memos, we looked for regularities and conditions that could explain and predict individual behaviour and justifications. We conducted an analysis of categories conditioned to individual living conditions (contextual and individual) and analysed elementary linkages between categories (see Huber, 1995; Prein, Kelle & Bird, 1995).

4. Results

All the interviewees agreed that they felt no moral dilemma about obtaining music by alternative means, but had different opinions about which approaches were morally acceptable and different arguments to justify their choices. This meant that certain behaviours were considered ethically justifiable in specific social, cultural and economic contexts (what Hayek called "living conditions"; see Gick, 2003) but not in other contexts. The moral arguments used to justify the same action thus varied according to context. Differences, in fact, seemed to crystallize around the social, cultural and economic background of the interviewees in childhood and around their current social position in terms of economic and cultural resources.

Figure 1 depicts the causal link between context and individual capital and their influence on behaviour.

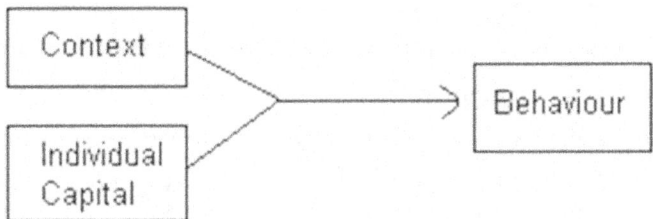

Figure 1. Theoretical links between context, individual capital and behaviour

The moral justification for accessing music by alternative means was contextual, that is, the issue of right or wrong depended on specific times and places. For example, materially developed countries typically have a broad range of audiovisual material available for borrowing from public libraries; consequently, given that access to culture is more universal, this access is perceived as a right guaranteed by society to individuals. Living conditions affect individual disposition and habits and, therefore, interpretation of personal behaviour and appropriate actions (Bourdieu, 1984).

In Spain in 2002, heavy use was being made of the generous stock of audiovisual material available from public libraries in large cities; according to López-Manzanedo (2003), 23.6% of all loans from Madrid's public libraries were of music CDs. In Barcelona's public libraries, CDs of various genres (traditional, jazz, pop-rock, classical, experimental and children's music) represent 10% of collections, although availability of more recent titles is an acknowledged difficulty. Libraries are nowadays a collective solution to the private problem of accessing culture. However, people in less developed countries must seek individual solutions for accessing music because few, if any, public alternatives are available.

Surprisingly, when we started to segment, code and categorize the interviews, we found that people from Chile did not slot into the logical divide between European and Latin American contexts, as they had, in fact, moral arguments and behaviour that were more akin to the Europeans than the Latin Americans in our sample. Further research on how CDs were produced and marketed in Latin America revealed that Chile was more similar to Europe in this respect. Furthermore, Chilean living conditions are also more similar to those in Europe than in other Latin American countries (Jaramillo, 2006). Consequently, we reformulated context from a geographical/cultural dimension to one representing personal living conditions; thus, Chilean, Greek and Spanish interviewees were classified as living in contexts with abundant public resources, while the rest of the interviewees (Argentinian, Bulgarian, Brazilian and Mexican) were classified as living in contexts with scarce public resources.

4.1. Different Contexts, Different Morally Acceptable Ways of Accessing Music

Consumers traditionally have accessed music by conventional exchanges in the music market. The record industry (through distributors and retailers) offers its products in the marketplace and consumers purchase the product provided that their willingness to pay is equal or superior to the price set by record firms or retailers. This is referred to as negotiated exchange, which can also occur in the informal economy. An alternative is referred to in terms of generalized exchange structures (Yamagishi & Cook, 1993). In this kind of exchange, benefits (in our case, music) flow to and from different actors. Participation requires each member to provide resources and to receive benefits over time, but not necessarily consistent with the member's offer. Trust is a vital component in the proper functioning of these structures, which are referred to as personally generalized exchanges when established among friends, as locally generalized exchanges when based on public libraries and as globally generalized exchanges when established through Internet social networks.

Fortunately — as will be seen below — our sample was diverse enough to determine the importance of social, cultural and economic contexts in terms of choosing one of these alternatives for accessing music.

When public resources are abundant, only generalized exchanges are viewed as morally acceptable. Individuals socialized in contexts where public resources were abundant preferred collective solutions to the private problem of music access.

Sara, a 25-year-old Spaniard with limited economic and cultural capital, clearly drew an analogy between music obtained from public libraries and from P2P networks on the Internet, but felt that the Internet offered more convenient access, greater variety and products not available in libraries or stores, including more live recordings of concerts and collaborations among artists:

"In the past I would go to the library to get some CDs (I still go to Caixa Forum to get CDs) and give them to a friend with a computer, he'd make me a copy or something... and now... if you can download it, it's ok because there are different things like... live concerts or lots of singers singing along with other singers... more concerts and more compilations and things you probably can't find at the library. Plus, it's more varied..." (Sara, para. 94)

Similar to Sara, Dolores (born in Chile but temporarily living in Barcelona) accessed music through the three forms of generalized exchange, that is, the Internet, public libraries and friends:

"Since I came to Barcelona, I've been downloading from the Internet. I bought a laptop computer within the first 3 or 4 months and got Internet access. Then I started to download music, not right away, but after a couple of months. I wasn't really sure about it, but once I'd started, I couldn't stop. It's simply a resource. Besides downloading from Internet, another resource is borrowing from a friend with an album: he lends it to me and I copy it onto the computer, but I don't copy the music onto a CD, just the computer... sometimes I go to the library to get a CD." (Dolores, para. 66)

In contexts with scarce public resources, negotiated exchanges in the informal economy and generalized exchanges are both considered to be morally acceptable. Interviewees from countries such as Brazil and Mexico could not consider public resources to be an alternative means for accessing music, as these resources were practically non-existent in their countries. They did, however, purchase illegal copies in the informal market. In Spain, this informal market is called *top manta* (Jaramillo, 2006), because the CDs are placed on a blanket (*manta*) that is used to gather up the merchandise when the police arrive, allowing the vendor to escape. Llomár (Brazil) and Carlos (Mexico) stated that buying illegal CDs was common in their countries and that they continued buying them in this way in Spain; they complained, however, that the variety of CDs offered in Spain was limited and too commercial compared with what was offered in their own countries:

"In Brazil it's very common, well it's not legal, it's illegal in Brazil. Policemen are all over it, but the way they're on the beach [illegal sellers]... well, on the beach there are plenty of people selling these CDs. If I like one and it's very cheap [I buy it]" (Llomár, para. 227)

"Here (in Barcelona) [I don't buy] a lot because they don't have... I already have the music that's available or I don't like it... In Mexico, there's a lot more variety in music." (Carlos, para. 63-65)

Some interviewees justified the purchase of illegal CDs on the basis of the social benefit it generated, as the copy and sale of such CDs creates an informal economy and so provides income for many families as well as a solution to the private problem of music access. In keeping with his local viewpoint, Carlos stressed personal benefits (convenience and financial accessibility) over collective ones (financial sustenance of the seller):

"It's more accessible than... buying from a store. I support these people, right? I don't know how many people live from this, but the trade seems more honest like this. I am helping the person from whom I buy the CD..." (Carlos, para. 100)

In contexts of abundant public resources, negotiated exchanges in the informal economy are morally wrong. Individuals socialized in contexts with abundant public resources and with access to culture did not value the fact that many families survive thanks to the sale of unauthorized copies of albums. The social structure of the informal economy, however, changes depending on the material development of the country in question. In Chile,

Spain and many other European countries, the activities of production (large-scale burning of unauthorized CDs) and marketing are performed by different actors: illegal and hidden organizations burn CDs whereas illegal immigrants run the risk of selling them in the streets. On the other hand, in Mexico, Brazil and other Latin American countries, CD production and marketing is done by families within the same country (Bishop, 2002).

These social differences in how production is organized probably affect the quality and diversity of the CDs offered. The internalization of production and marketing increases the incentives for greater variety (adapted to local tastes) and quality control (sellers sometimes even offer their mobile number in case a customer is not satisfied with the product; see Jaramillo, 2006):

> *"[Top mantas] also are in fully equipped places... with woofer and ceiling, they have electricity and a sound device to test [the CDs]... it's very common."* (Carlos, para. 306)

In contexts of abundant public resources, centralized production and variations in seller identity do not favour either the quality or variety of the unauthorized CDs offered for sale. Furthermore, individuals in this context have more collective options for accessing culture: friends have more music and libraries have large and varied collections of music and videos. For Sara, it was very clear: rather than buy from *top mantas* she would borrow the album from a friend. Ana, also Spanish, used a legal argument to justify her behaviour: selling unauthorized albums is a crime because the seller profits from the work of others, whereas making copies for private use from originals obtained from public or private sources (libraries, friends or the Internet) does not imply financial profit and so should not be illegal. Borrowing from the library was considered, in fact, to be similar to downloading music:

> *"Instead of buying it from top mantas, I ask a friend to copy it and nothing else. I've never bought from top mantas."* (Sara, para. 136)

> "(...) in a way it seems wrong.... I don't buy pirated music for example ... I don't want to buy it, so I download it ..., It can't be legal, but because of this market situation of downloading music... which is not a crime, but selling is, right?" (Ana, para. 166-172)

Depending on the context, people viewed the seller differently, that is, as "one of us" or "one of them". In countries where unauthorized CDs are largely sold by immigrants, consumers considered that purchase was illegal, whereas this was largely untrue for countries where production and marketing is carried out by families of the same nationality.

In fact, in contexts with scarce public resources for accessing culture, buying unauthorized music is not necessarily perceived as legally suspect because many families sell music from stands with a basic infrastructure (for instance, with an electricity supply). This transmits the message that they are accepted by society in general, so selling unauthorized copies in this way tells people that purchase is socially acceptable. In contexts of abundant public resources, however, the fact that unauthorized copies are sold by immigrants in the streets enhances the perception of immorality in the eyes of society.

4.2. Different Contexts, Different Moral Arguments to Justify Behaviours

Fair use. The issue of fair use raises two issues, firstly that of making copies for one's own use, and secondly, that of the right to be able to access a few tracks without being obliged to purchase an entire CD.

Fair use is a social contract that recognizes creator and record industry rights to claim compensation for their productions and also individual rights to access culture. For instance, Spanish Law 23/2006, of 7 July, governing intellectual property (Official State Gazette, 8 July 2006) regulates fair use of private copies as follows (Article 31.2): "No authorization need be obtained from the author for the reproduction of promulgated works in any medium by a natural person for private use, provided the works have been accessed legally and the copy obtained is not used for collective or for-profit use, and without prejudice to the fair compensation set forth in Article 25, which shall be taken into consideration if the measures mentioned in Article 161 are applied to such works."

In regard to private copying, moral arguments differed depending on the context. Thus, interviewees socialized in a context of abundant public resources for accessing culture were of the opinion that the private use of downloaded copies was fair use because they did not sell the music and only searched for tracks, not entire albums. In fact, these particular interviewees had internalized their right of access to culture, given that they were accustomed to obtaining music from public libraries.

Interviewees extended the right to make private copies for personal use to copying from friends, the radio, television, libraries and the Internet. A right was also perceived in terms of making private copies of music purchased in the formal market. Record publishers, however, restrict the right to make private copies of legally owned albums by applying copyright protection (such as watermarks) to CDs. Owners are thus only allowed to make a limited number of copies or are limited as to the kind of device they use to play songs (for instance, iPod for music purchased through iTunes):

> "(...) this is not a job for me. I mean, I download things for myself. I don't sell them and I don't make them available to anyone, nothing of the sort. It's simply for me, for my own use, like buying an original album. I would record it for myself and keep it in the car. Well, it's the same, it doesn't leave this place." (Jean, para. 88)

This group of interviewees was more aware of the legal consequences of copying original productions for personal use and using productions not purchased in the market:

> "But you know what you are risking, I mean, the moment you make a copy, if you have the original there's no problem because in an inspection or whatever... you can show the CD you used, meaning you can show the copy and the original from which you made it. So, in this case, they can't do anything. But when you make a copy and you

don't have the original, then you can have a problem because they can really hurt you." (Joan, para. 160)

In terms of the right of access to specific tracks without having to buy the entire CD, sharing songs was considered fair because in many cases a consumer might like just one or two tracks from a CD and so it was viewed as unfair to be forced to buy the entire CD. Many consumers recall the option that formerly existed of being able to buy a 45-rpm record (single) with only two songs as an alternative to buying a full 33-rpm long-playing record (LP). The interviewees perceived their behaviour to be morally acceptable because music labels no longer offer singles (and, although this is now possible through digital sites such as iTunes, not all record labels market productions in this way). In fact, consumers consider music downloading (from the Internet) or copying (from friends or libraries) analogous to photocopying chapters of books borrowed from libraries. Many publishers accept this practice as fair use and have set higher prices for journal subscriptions and hardcover books in order to account for the expected value of future copying of articles or chapters, independently of the number of copies:

> "Because this was not obligatory in the past. In the past they used to produce singles that were, for example, 45 [rpm] records; they produced records with only one song. That's not true any longer. Now, they want you to listen to the entire record and I don't feel that's fair. They don't even try to remedy the situation so that people can buy only one song. When a really good song comes out (...) they make thousands of copies of the record, but [referring to record industries] make a copy so that people can buy that specific song and won't have to look for it on the Internet. I mean [they should] make it easier instead of... blaming the people who download music." (Jean, para. 213)

Taking advantage of the situation. Interviewees who had less personal capital or who came from a background of scarce public resources did not use fair use arguments to justify their behaviour. Rather, they typically emphasized how the situation benefited them personally, with each individual taking advantage of the opportunities provided by technology and blaming record labels for unsuitable policies. These interviewees made the most of the existing situation, with no signs of regret other than vague misgivings about the financial consequences for artists:

> "The truth is that I never pirate on the Internet, I mean that I don't feel guilty and I don't see it like that. I've never really thought about it seriously, I mean, I've never really thought, "No, I am not going to do it." I mean, it was always "Ah, great, I have free music" (...) If I can have the same product without paying, why should I pay? (...) Some people have criteria of an ethical nature, which is on another level. Thinking that I'm stealing or ripping off artists or stuff like that, but at a financial level, is as simple as... as buying a can of olives at a better price." (José, para. 102, 116)

The main justification was based on the availability of more economic alternatives for accessing music (that is, accessing music at the least possible cost), rather than any consideration of right or wrong. For this reason, these users copied music so as to exploit what they considered to be a temporary situation. Whereas moral reasoning seemed to be a luxury available to those who could afford it, the problem for some individuals was simply how to obtain music, not whether or not it was morally right to access music. This access argument becomes more evident when the cost of a CD and wages for different countries are compared, using Brazil and the USA as an illustrative example (see Bishop, 2002: pages 8-9). The minimum monthly wage in Brazil in 2002 was around R$ 200 and a CD cost R$ 24.90; the corresponding wage in the USA was US$ 892.66 and a CD cost $ 17.99. Thus, in Brazil a CD cost around 12% of the minimum monthly wage, compared to just 2% in the USA:

> "Here I think it is more like a...a first world country, it's a lot closer to the consumer trends that exist in the USA, where buying a CD according to the income per capita, the money a family has available or the budget...of a student is affordable... like teens who

buy, for example, clothes, music and have money for it. But in my country... it's not that way. In the sense... that music is more expensive." (Jorge, para. 213)

Apart from taking advantage of the situation, interviewees eluded personal responsibility by arguing that if downloading was possible, then it was because it was allowed. In a way, they waived any responsibility for deciding what was right or wrong by assigning the blame to record labels who have allowed the expansion of P2P programs:

"*If music is on websites for us, we download it. We have no reason not to. It's easy, it's safe.*" (Llomár, para. 164)

"*You don't know if it's legal or illegal. You just found it, you do it and that's all.*" (Albert, para. 189)

4.3. Different Contexts, Different Predispositions to Change Behaviour

Changes in behaviour will depend on the consequences. It would seem that changes in the future behaviour of the interviewees would depend on the social, cultural and economic context. In a context of abundant public resources individuals make a trade-off between the convenience and variety offered by the Internet and the public access offered by libraries. If downloading music from the Internet meant high fines, these interviewees would be likely to modify their behaviour and turn to the traditional public alternatives (borrowing from libraries or from friends). The availability of public alternatives reduced dependence on negotiated exchanges in the formal and informal markets. Individuals who understood how P2P networks operate felt safer because it was unlikely they would be tracked down by the industry, given the enormous number of peers all over the world and the anonymity provided by these programs. Thus, calculating the benefits and costs of each alternative, they chose the one that in the end made them feel safest:

"It depends on whether they would fine me or not. It would be best for me... to wait. I'm a member of a library and at Caixa Forum there's plenty of music. But, no, I think that if they really are that civic-minded, maybe... well,... I don't know... It depends on how expensive the fine would be and on whether I could pay it. I might keep on downloading if it's not very expensive... Maybe I would pay it because they can't see everything on the Internet. I mean, I think they can't really know who you are. It's not that controlled..." (Sara, para. 126)

"Man... I would download a lot less... and I would think a lot about what I would or wouldn't download. I'd have to see if I like the music or not, and if I do, well, then I could buy it." (Albert, para. 198-199)

"The Internet provides anonymity for those who can protect themselves and understand the possibilities of the Internet, so they can't be seen anywhere. There are programs and users who are watching everything that goes on over the Internet; if someone knows how, they can avoid it." (Christos, para. 140)

Some interviewees drew an analogy with similar cases (such as Spanish interviewees with the law against smoking in public and private establishments), believing that the informal economy would continue to exist even despite a response by record labels. Interviewees did, however, seem to draw a clear distinction between the reactions of people in the USA and in Europe. They accepted the need for legal safeguards, but also believed that music downloading from the Internet should be permitted. Europeans, interviewees suggest, would strongly oppose any effort to prohibit downloading, as they believed that consumer coalitions would be formed to influence politicians and prevent music downloading for private use from being considered a criminal act:

"I don't know. That's the problem. You don't know until the moment comes. It's the same with the smoking law. Until it was applied, we didn't know. All the people (said) 'Oh, I don't know, when the law

comes... It came, they smoke less. They will also download less, but they will download." (Joan, para. 175-176)

"I'd consider [not downloading]. But it'd make me really angry. In this regard, I think they're more progressive here. I think that there would be some kind of mobilization; in fact, there are issues of mobilization in Europe, things that don't happen in the USA. So I guess that people would react and claim rights, and I think that they wouldn't [bring lawsuits] in the end. If it came to that, I guess I would think about it, and yeah, I would stop doing it to avoid running a risk... so I'd compromise like everyone else or I'd run the risk and compromise in that way..." (Inés, para. 144)

As long as no alternatives exist, consumers will continue to download or buy music in the informal market. It seems that individuals socialized in a context with scarce public resources for accessing culture would continue downloading music. On the one hand, they do not believe that record publishers would react the same way in Europe, given the likelihood of public mobilization that would limit the powers of the record industry. Some European countries have already started imposing legislation, however; France, for example, introduced a new regulation in 2007 that imposes fines for downloading music from the Internet. The same individuals passed on the responsibility for what they did to other individuals or to P2P programs that facilitate music downloads. This strategy is also used by record labels and copyright associations against P2P providers, but for different reasons; they would like providers of downloading services to be obliged to identify the peers — which would be more cost effective for them than acting against individual consumers:

"I won't stop downloading... if there are really open Internet sites where people can enter, I don't see that they can do it. I'll keep on downloading music because it is just like entering a forum and passing on something, right? If the moderator forbids you from entering, you can't enter the forum, for example, you can't write. It's the same with

IPs and so on. Of course, it's everyone in that forum... I only see that if everyone does things that are, let's say, illegal, what can you do except ban the entire forum and not simply deny entrance or sue a person... I guess fewer people would [download]." (Elena, para. 141-142)

5. Discussion and Conclusions

We have found that the morality of consumers regarding alternative ways to access music depended on the social background and personal capital (economic and cultural) of each person. Contrary to previous research (Kuo & Hsu, 2001; Xiaohe, 2006; Solomon & O'Brien, 1990; Cohen & Cornwell, 1989; Moore & McMullan, 2004; Lau, 2006; Husted, 2000), we allowed users from varied contextual settings and with different levels of personal capital to express their own moral arguments regarding their actions in accessing culture. Sample composition was sufficiently varied to make it clear that what was considered ethically right or wrong depended on an individual's sociocultural context and personal resources. Lack of sample variety is precisely why research to date has not been able to establish a relationship between the ethical scale used to represent moral stances and the copying of software or music for personal use. Our research shows that, in regard to alternative ways of accessing information goods, what is considered wrong by the music industry is not necessarily consistent with what consumers consider wrong. In fact, what consumers considered to be right or wrong varied according to the public resources available in terms of being able to access culture.

Taking into consideration that moral arguments depend on the actual context in which an individual has been raised, we agree with the logic of Swinyard et al. (1990) and Bishop (2002), which is that a comparison of social and economic contexts reveals major differences in motives. In earlier research, sociocultural contexts were too similar (undergraduate and graduate students in the USA and the general population in China) to enable differences to be detected in the behaviours that consumers considered right or wrong and why.

Although previous research has shown a connection between software copying and moral values (Logsdon et al., 1994), demographics and social norms (Moore & McMullan, 2004; Simpson et al., 1994; Al-Jabri & Abdul-Gader, 1997), knowledge of computers (Taylor & Shim, 1993; Oz, 2001; Wagner & Sanders, 2001) and personal benefits (Swinyard et al., 1990; Glass & Wood, 1996), we have focused on investigating the social and economic reasons that make it ethical — in consumers' minds — to consume music obtained by alternative means. In the field of research into music consumption to date, only the economic factor has been investigated as a key motivation (Bishop, 2002; Condry, 2004; Easley, 2005). In our study, however, we have also attempted to account for the influences of the cultural environments in which people develop their reasoning and in which they perform their acts.

Our different research design shows that, in contexts with abundant public resources, an option exists for accessing music other than the market-based exchange offered by major record labels, namely, the public library, mostly used by people with low levels of economic capital. This option significantly lowers the dependency of individuals on the record industry. In contexts with scarce public resources, however, the only formal alternative is the purchase of original CDs at almost the same nominal price as in richer markets, and, in real terms this makes a CD far more expensive in relative income terms than in more developed economies.

Structured according to context (abundant versus scarce public resources) and personal resources (high versus low capital), we delineate two models, one describing music access behaviours (Table 2) and the other describing the moral arguments given by people to justify these behaviours (Table 3). Thus, Table 2 shows that, in a context of abundant public resources — regardless of personal resources — people have a preference for sharing music over the Internet or among friends. Only people with high economic capital typically purchase original CDs, and, although people with less economic capital do buy originals (when discounted), they typically prefer to borrow from friends or public libraries. In contexts of scarce public resources, irrespective of whether they have high or low personal resources, consumers usually buy illegal CDs or borrow CDs from friends. Only consumers with enough economic capital download music from the Internet or purchase CDs in the formal market.

Table 2. Music access: behaviours according to personal resources and context*

	Context	
Personal resources	Abundant public resources	Scarce public resources
High	• Loans from friends • Downloads from the Internet • Formal purchases	• Informal purchases • Loans from friends • Downloads from the Internet • Formal purchases
Low	• Loans from friends • Loans from libraries • Downloads from the Internet • Formal purchases	• Informal purchases • Loans from friends

*Behaviours are listed in order of importance.

Moral arguments are summarized in Table 3. People living in contexts with abundant public resources typically acquire original CDs for their symbolic value but also defend their right to access music in accordance with the fair use argument. Users in this context also agree that they use the Internet fairly (copies are for personal use and access is usually to few tracks in an album). However, differences appear in the moral arguments concerning music downloads, with people with high personal capital arguing that they can obtain music not available in stores, and people with low personal capital saying that they were taking advantage of the situation. In contexts of scarce public resources, moral arguments are identical for users with high and low personal resources: purchasing illegal CDs, helping people make a living and taking advantage of the situation (whether by downloading or copying from friends).

Table 3. *Music access: moral arguments according to personal resources and context**

Personal resources	Context	
	Abundant public resources	**Scarce public resources**
High	• Original purchased for its symbolic properties • Fair use: copies for personal use • Fair use: music not available in stores	• Purchasing illegal CDs and helping people make a living • Taking advantage of the situation: borrowing from friends • Taking advantage of the situation: downloading
Low	• Original purchased for its symbolic properties • Fair use: copies for personal use • Taking advantage of the situation: downloading	• Purchasing illegal CDs and helping people make a living • Taking advantage of the situation: borrowing from friends • Taking advantage of the situation: downloading

*Moral arguments are listed in order of importance.

Our findings suggest that in contexts with abundant public resources, buying CDs in the informal economy is considered morally wrong, whereas the general opinion is the opposite in contexts with scarce public resources. Institutionally, the practice of buying CDs in the informal economy differed between contexts: (1) in contexts with abundant public resources, this practice was looked down on because of questionable production (by illegal firms) and sale (by immigrants) practices for illegal and unreliable CDs limited in variety; and (2) in contexts of scarce public resources, the production and marketing of unauthorized copies of CDs was a more familiar practice, with a greater variety of more reliable CDs (which, moreover, helped people make a living). These differences in how production and marketing are organized socially clearly influence ethical interpretations in regard to buying unauthorized albums. Differences in incomes and in the availability of public resources thus largely explain differences in what people consider to be ethically right or wrong.

Along with the individual's resources (economic and cultural), the social context also affects the moral arguments used to justify actions. In countries with abundant public resources, people justify their preference for downloading music as being similar to — but more convenient than — borrowing music from the library; it is also seen as a way to avoid being exploited by record labels when only one or a few tracks on an entire album are of interest. Apparently, it makes no moral difference to individuals how they obtained a free copy of an album: as an original or as a copy from friends, public libraries or the Internet. The positive outcome of having a copy is considered to be the opportunity to consume only the product they like and not the entire album purchased at what is perceived to be an extortionate price, as suggested by Condry (2004), Easley (2005) and Lau (2006). People raised in countries with scarce public resources, however, are not troubled by the morality of buying CDs in the informal market or downloading them from a P2P network (if they could afford an Internet connection), because they lack public alternatives. In this context, the only alternative to purchasing pricey original CDs is to obtain inexpensive or free copies. Individuals feel trapped when no authorized way to access music other than purchase exists, and so they opt for unauthorized ways to access music — a behaviour also reported by Swinyard et al. (1990) and Bishop (2002).

The morally acceptable nature of making private copies from the CDs of friends or from the radio has now extended to music downloads from the Internet, justified on the basis that users have no intention of gaining financial profit from a product they have not produced. Our interviewees did not view themselves as equivalent to illegal vendors in terms of motives or activity, but as fair users whose behaviour was morally acceptable. In particular, individuals living in a context of abundant public resources consider borrowing music from a public library to be similar to accessing music through P2P file-sharing networks, simply that the latter are more convenient and offer a larger music catalogue. For the same context, consumers with less economic capital who were less willing to pay for an original CD considered that downloading was a technological opportunity that they should exploit for as long as possible, believing that the option will eventually disappear when legal mechanisms are instituted by record labels. Users with more extensive computer skills felt that downloading was neither temporary (because of the growth in the practice) nor identifiable (because they knew how to avoid it) and so they felt relatively immune to punishment.

The availability of public resources and personal capital also divided interviewees when it came to the issue of changing behaviour in response to an hypothetical increase in penalties for using alternative ways to access music. Individuals in contexts of scarce public resources did not feel intimidated by the penalties announced by record industries, denying any intention of changing their behaviour — meaning that they planned to continue either downloading music or purchasing CDs in the informal economy. As with the case of the illegal vendor accused by the record industries of an illicit act, individuals pass the responsibility for downloading to the P2P software developers; this mentality underscores the individual nature of use in these contexts and imbues users with a sense of safety. Those who were more fortunate in public resource terms said they would stop downloading music if financial penalties were sufficiently high, probably because they live in a context that offers other options (such as public libraries) — a conclusion also drawn by Glass and Wood (1996).

Our findings also point to the fact that, in accessing music, individuals choose the means that best benefit them and that are morally consistent with their habits, in turn influenced by the sociocultural context in which they were raised and live in and also by their personal capital. Interestingly, social context interacts with individual economic and cultural capital, affecting consumer actions and the moral arguments used to justify these actions. In a theoretical framework, it seems that the social exchange theory (Emerson, 1962; Yamagishi & Cook, 1993) best describes individual decision making and behaviour evaluation, since it takes into account the subjective cost-benefit analysis performed by people when comparing alternatives. We have seen that in every context there is a clear distinction between a formal and an informal music market, with the form and size of the latter depending on the form and size of the former. The alternatives provided by the informal music market are simply a reaction to the choice (or lack of choice) offered by the formal market.

In sum, our findings suggest that samples of informants must be heterogeneous in order to be able to understand individual behaviour when accessing music using alternative means, given that individual actions and the arguments used to justify these actions are affected by contexts and personal circumstances. The theory emerging from our data suggests not only that the morality of actions for accessing culture by alternative means depends on the social, cultural, and economic context in which an individual operates, but also that an individual's social context interacts with their economic and cultural capital, and, ultimately, with the moral arguments used to justify specific actions. Necessary, however, is further research comparing producers and/or consumers in different social, cultural and economic contexts so as to identify new dimensions to moral reasoning and behaviour.

Throughout our research we have attempted to apply the guidelines proposed by Goetz and LeCompte (1988) in regard to improving the possibilities for replicating findings. We should mention, however, that, were other researchers to follow the same procedures described in this article, it would still be well nigh impossible to replicate the original conditions in which the data were collected (see Strauss & Corbin, 1991: page 266). This is because music is downloaded in many different social settings and has become universal. Nevertheless, another set of actions similar to music downloading (downloading software or other information goods) could theoretically replicate our research and generalize the theory (Seale, 1999). Our findings could thus be transferred to individuals raised in countries resembling the countries researched here, but if and only if, this transference was done purposefully to explain and predict behaviour and arguments supporting that behaviour. In other words, a theory could be developed by generalizing the substantive theory developed here to other substantive domains, such as, for example, software accessed using unconventional means.

Acknowledgements

This research has been possible thanks to funding from the Centre d'Estudis i de Recerca d'Humanitats (CERHUM) at the Universitat Autònoma de Barcelona, the European Union ERDF Programme and the Spanish Ministry of Education and Science (Research Project ECO2011-29558-C02-01-E) and the Catalan Autonomous Government/Agència de Gestió d'Ajuts Universitaris i de Recerca (AGAUR) (Grant 2014-SGR-502). We would also like to thank the informants who have helped us with our research by sharing with us a part of their lives.

References

Al-Jabri, I., & Abdul-Gader, A. (1997). Software Copyright Infringements: An Exploratory Study of the Effects of Individual and Peer Beliefs. *International Journal of Management Science*, 25(3): 335-344.
http://dx.doi.org/10.1016/s0305-0483(96)00053-9

Bishop, J. (2002). Politics of music piracy: A comparative look at Brazil and the United States. *47th Annual Meeting of the Society for Ethnomusicology*, Estes Park, Colorado, 24 October.

Bourdieu, P. (1984). *Distinction: a social critique of the judgment of taste*. London: Routledge.

Charmaz, K. (2000). Grounded Theory: Objectivist and Constructivist Methods. In Denzin, N.K., & Lincoln, Y.S. (Eds.). *Handbook of Qualitative Research* (2nd edition). London: Sage.

Cohen, E., & Cornwell, L. (1989). College students believe piracy is acceptable. *CIS Educator Forum: A Quarterly Journal*, 1(3), 2-5.

Condry, I. (2004). Cultures of music piracy: An ethnographic comparison of the US and Japan. *International Journal of Cultural Studies*, 7(3), 343-363.
http://dx.doi.org/10.1177/1367877904046412

Coyle, J.R., Gould, S.J., Gupta, P., & Gupta, R. (2009). To buy or to pirate: the matrix of music consumers' acquisition-mode decision–making. *Journal of Business Research*, 62, 1031-1037.

http://dx.doi.org/10.1016/j.jbusres.2008.05.002

Denzin, K.N., & Lincoln, S.L. (1994). *Handbook of Qualitative Research*. Thousand Oaks, CA: Sage.

Denzin, N.K. (1989). *Interpretive Interactionism*. Newbury Park: Sage.

Easley, R.F. (2005). Ethical issues in the music industry, response to innovation and piracy. *Journal of Business Ethics*, 62, 163-168.

http://dx.doi.org/10.1007/s10551-005-0187-3

Emerson, R.M. (1962). Power-dependence relations. *American Sociological Review* 27(1), 31-41.

http://dx.doi.org/10.2307/2089716

Gick, E. (2003). Cognitive theory and moral behavior: the contribution of F.A. Hayek to Business Ethics. *Journal of Business Ethics*, 45, 149-165.

http://dx.doi.org/10.1023/A:1024141017104

Giddens, A. (1976). *New Rules of Sociological Method: A Positive Critique of Interpretative Sociologies*. London: Hutchinson.

Giesler, M., & Pohlmann, M. (2003), The anthropology of file-sharing: consuming Napster as a gift. *Advances in Consumer Research*, 30, 1-7.

Glaser, B.G., & Strauss, A.L. (1967. *The Discovery of Grounded Theory: Strategies for Qualitative Research*. Chicago: Aldine.

Glaser, B.G. (1978). *Theoretical Sensitivity: Advances in the Methodology of Grounded Theory*. Mill Valley, CA: Sociology Press.

Glass, S., & Wood, A.W. (1996). Situational determinants of software piracy: an equity theory perspective. *Journal of Business Ethics*, 15(11), 1189-1198.

http://dx.doi.org/10.1007/BF00412817

Goetz, J.P., & Lecompte, M.D. (1988). *Etnografía y diseño cualitativo en investigación educativa*. Madrid: Morata (Trans: Antonio Ballesteros).

Goulding, C. (2000). The museum environment and the visitors' experience. *European Journal of Marketing*, 34(3/4), 271-278.

http://dx.doi.org/10.1108/03090560010311849

Hendry, J. (2001). After Durkheim: an agenda for the sociology of business ethics. *Journal of Business Ethics*, 34, 209-218.

http://dx.doi.org/10.1023/A:1012558717452

Huber, G. (1995). Qualitative hypothesis examination and theory building. In Kelle, U. (Ed.). *Computer-Aided Qualitative Data Analysis: Theory, Methods and Practice*. London: Sage. 136-151.

Husted, W.B. (2000). The impact of national culture on software piracy. *Journal of Business Ethics*, 26, 197-211.

http://dx.doi.org/10.1023/A:1006250203828

Jaramillo, B. (2006). Mi cultura pirate. 27 August. *La Nación-Domingo.*
http://www.lanacion.cl/noticias/reportaje/mi-cultura-pirata/2006-08-26/182729.html

Kelle, U., & Laurie, H. (1995). Computer use in qualitative research and issues of validity. In Kelle, U. (Ed.). *Computer-Aided Qualitative Data Analysis: Theory, Methods and Practice.* London: Sage. 19-28.

Kuo, F.Y., & Hsu, M.H. (2001). Development and validation of ethical computer self-efficacy measure: the case of soft lifting. *Journal of Business Ethics.* 32(4), 299-315.
http://dx.doi.org/10.1023/A:1010715504824

Lau, E.K. (2006). Factors motivating people toward pirated software. *Qualitative Market Research: An International Journal,* 9(4), 404-419.
http://dx.doi.org/10.1108/13522750610689113

Lee, G.M., & Eining, M.M. & Long, C.P. (1994). Information ethics: a comparative among college students from Mainland China, Hong Kong and Taiwan. *Hong Kong Journal of Business Management,* 12, 17-35.

Logsdon, J.M., Thompson, J.K., & Reid, R.A. (1994). Software piracy: is it related to level of moral judgment? *Journal of Business Ethics,* 13(11), 849-857.
http://dx.doi.org/10.1007/BF00871698

López-Manzanedo, M.J. (2003). Las bibliotecas públicas en España: visión general. *2nd International Meeting of Public Libraries.* Puerto Vallarta (Mexico).

Moore, R., & McMullan, E.C. (2004). Perceptions of peer-to-peer file sharing among university students. *Journal of Criminal Justice and Popular Culture,* 11(1), 1-19.

Oz, E. (2001). Organizational commitment and ethical behaviour: an empirical study of information system professionals. *Journal of Business Ethics,* 34(2), 137-146.
http://dx.doi.org/10.1023/A:1012214017119

Patton, M.Q. (2002). *Qualitative research and evaluation methods* (3rd edition). Thousand Oakes, CA: Sage.

Peace, A.G. (1997). Software piracy and computer using professionals: a survey. *Journal of Computer Information Systems,* 37(3), 94-99.

Peterson, R.A. (1990). Why 1955? *Popular Music,* 9, 97-116.
http://dx.doi.org/10.1017/S0261143000003767

Peterson, R.A. (1997). *Creating Country Music: Fabricating Authenticity.* Chicago: University of Chicago Press.

Peterson, R.A., & Berger, D. (1975). Cycles in symbolic production: The case of popular music. *American Sociological Review,* 40, 158-173.
http://dx.doi.org/10.2307/2094343

Prein, G., Kelle, U. & Bird, K. (1995). An overview of software. In Kelle, U. (Ed.). *Computer-aided Qualitative Data Analysis: Theory, Methods and Practice.* London: Sage. 190-210.

Richards, T., & Richards, L. (1995). Using hierarchical categories in qualitative data analysis. In Kelle, U. (Ed.). *Computer-Aided Qualitative Data Analysis: Theory, Methods and Practice*. London: Sage. 80-95.

Seale, C. (1999). *The Quality of Qualitative Research*. London: Sage

Shang, R., Chen, Y., & Chen, P. (2007). Ethical decisions about sharing music files in the P2P environment. *Journal of Business Ethics*, 80, 349-365.

http://dx.doi.org/10.1007/s10551-007-9424-2

Simpson, P.M., Banerjee, D., & Simpson Jr., C.I. (1994). Soft lifting: a model of motivating factor. *Journal of Business Ethics*, 15(8), 431-438.

http://dx.doi.org/10.1007/BF00881451

Sims, R.R., Cheng, H.K., & Teegen, H. (1996). Toward a Profile of Student Software Piraters. *Journal of Business Ethics*, 15(8), 839-849.

http://dx.doi.org/10.1007/BF00381852

Solomon, S.L., & O'Brien, J. A. (1990). The effect of demographic factors on attitudes toward software piracy. *Journal of Computer Information Systems*, 30(3), 41-46.

Spitz, D., & Hunter, S.D. (2005). Contested codes: the social construction of Napster. *The Information Society*, 21, 1-27.

http://dx.doi.org/10.1080/01972240490951890

Strauss, A. (1987). *Qualitative Analysis for Social Scientists*. Cambridge: Cambridge University Press.

http://dx.doi.org/10.1017/CBO9780511557842

Strauss, A., & Corbin, J. (1991). *Basics of Qualitative Research*. London: Sage.

Swinyard, W.R., Rinne, H., & Kau, A.K. (1990). The morality of software piracy: a cross-cultural analysis. *Journal of Business Ethics*, 9, 655-664.

http://dx.doi.org/10.1007/BF00383392

Taylor, G.S., & Shim, J.P. (1993). A comparative examination toward software piracy among business professors and executives. *Human Relations*, 46, 419-433.

http://dx.doi.org/10.1177/001872679304600401

Thong, Y.L., & Yap, C.S. (1998). Testing an ethical decision-making theory: the case of soft lifting. *Journal of Management Information Systems*, 15(1), 213-237.

http://dx.doi.org/10.1080/07421222.1998.11518203

Tschudi, F. (1989). Do qualitative and quantitative methods require the same approach to validity? In Kvale, S. (Ed.). *Issues of Validity in Qualitative Research*. Lund: Studentlitteratur. 109-134.

Wagner, S.C., & Sanders, G.L. (2001). Considerations in Ethical Decision Making. *The Journal of Business Ethics*, 29 (1, 2), 161-167.

http://dx.doi.org/10.1023/A:1006415514200

Wilson, T.P. (1970). Conceptions of interaction and forms of sociological explanation *American Journal of Sociology*, 35(4), 697-710.

http://dx.doi.org/10.2307/2093945

Xiaohe, L. (2006). On P2P File-Sharing: A Major Problem – A Chinese Perspective. *Journal of Business Ethics*, 63(1), 63-73.

http://dx.doi.org/10.1007/s10551-005-1130-3

Yamagishi, T., & Cook, K.S. (1993). Generalized Exchange and Social Dilemmas. *Social Psychology Quarterly*, 56(4), 235-248.

http://dx.doi.org/10.2307/2786661

Chapter 6

Music access patterns: A social interpretation based on consumption volume and linkage needs[*]

Jordi López-Sintas[1], Àngel Cebollada-Frontera[1], Nela Filimon[2], Abaghan Ghahraman[1]

[1]Universitat Autònoma de Barcelona, Spain.
[2]Universitat de Girona, Spain.

jordi.lopez@uab.es, Angel.Cebollada@uab.cat, nela.filimon@udg.edu, abaghan.ghahraman@uab.cat

Doi: http://dx.doi.org/10.3926/oms.303

How to cite this chapter

López-Sintas, J., Cebollada-Frontera, À., Filimon, N. Ghahraman A. (2015). Music access patterns: A social interpretation based on consumption volume and linkage needs. In López-Sintas, J. (Ed.). *The social construction of culture markets: Between incentives to creation and access to culture.* Barcelona, Spain: OmniaScience. pp. 161-208.

---

[*] This chapter (a longer version of the article published in *Poetics*, Volume 46, October 2014, pp. 56-74) is reproduced with kind permission from Elsevier.

J. López-Sintas, À. Cebollada-Frontera, N. Filimon, A. Ghahraman

Abstract

The substitution of purchased music by downloaded music has been much researched using individualistic psychological or economic frameworks. However, such research designs rarely take into account the social dimension of music taste and access to music, with social science research only recently addressing the way individuals access information and cultural expressions. Our research develops and tests a theoretical model of access to music that is based on the life stage and social position of individuals (as reflected by their age and education) and explains why and how music access patterns, motivations and listening behaviours are structured by both these factors.

Keywords

Music access pattern, motivation, music consumption, theory of music access, latent class analysis.

1. Introduction

Music tastes have been extensively researched and, according to Bennett, Emmisson and Frow (1999: page 171), have acquired the status of "sensitive barometers of more general cultural dispositions". In his famous work *Distinction,* Bourdieu states that "nothing more clearly affirms one's class, nothing more infallibly classifies, than tastes in music" (1984: page 18). However, individuals have to access music before they can enjoy and develop any particular tastes. Access is therefore a broader concept than market exchange (Belk, 2013). By access to music we refer to how individuals nowadays get music, which may be through traditional physical exchanges or digital exchanges, either of which can be market or social exchanges. Even though the way people access culture has changed radically in recent years, this issue has been much less investigated than tastes in music.

Most of the existing research addressing how individuals access music has adopted either an economic or psychological framework. The economic framework explores the impact of Internet file sharing (digital social exchanges among unknown peers) on falling music purchases (market exchanges), whereas the psychological framework attempts to explain individual factors (motivations, benefits, perceptions, ethics, personal attachment to artists, etc) that correlate with Internet file sharing and music purchases. Findings regarding the economic impact of Internet file sharing on music industry sales have been rather mixed (Liebowitz, 2005; Liebowitz & Watt, 2006; Michel, 2004). Research based on the psychological framework, which has not been any more fructiferous, has only rarely tended to focus on social indicators for the sampled individuals (Sandulli, 2007; Wang, Chen, Yang & Farn, 2009).

Social researchers have recently started to describe the way individuals access information and cultural expressions using the Internet (a medium for the digital social exchange of culture). Kayahara and Wellman (2007), for instance, studied a sample of Canadians searching for information about culture; Nieckarz Jr. (2005) researched the role of the Internet in facilitating and maintaining a community that collects and trades live-music performances (a digital social exchange); Tepper, Hargittai and Touve (2007) and Tepper and Hargittai (2009) studied the music exploration pathways used by university students (traditional and digital exchanges of information); and Williams (2006) studied the roles played by live music and the Internet (traditional and digital exchanges) in self-identifying members of the straightedge youth subculture. Results point to the important role played by peers in terms of selecting kinds of culture expressions and by the Internet in terms of accessing further information.

Rather than focus on substitution between ways of accessing music or on the relationship between information sources and ways of accessing culture, our research explores social patterns of how and why people access music. More specifically, we endeavour to provide evidence and a social interpretation that could go some way to explaining associations between age and music access and between music access and social position. If music taste is a social classifier — as argued by Bourdieu (1984), by Bennett et al. (1999) and by Williams (2006) — then we may ask ourselves: are music access patterns not also socially structured?

To answer this question, we used a nationally representative Spanish microdata sample and a relational methodology that combined latent class modelling and correspondence analysis in order to, first, identify music access patterns and, second, determine the relationship between these patterns and several sets of indicators. We identified four broad consumer groups: *non-accessers*, who never bought, copied or downloaded any music whatsoever; *buyers*, who generally preferred to purchase music; and two intermediate groups, namely, *downloaders*, who predominantly downloaded music from peer-to-peer (P2P) networks, and *copiers-buyers*, who typically copied from friends/family but also purchased music. Each music access pattern was socially structured by age and by social position, as were the volumes listened to and individual motivations.

2. Theoretical Music Access Framework

2.1. Findings for an Individualistic Framework

Our understanding of who (social interpretation of behaviour) accesses music, and how (behaviour patterns) and why (motivations) they do so, is rather limited. Researchers have, nonetheless, studied the impact of background and motivations on the ways consumers access music, paying special attention to: (1) patterns of accessing music; (2) the impact of downloading music from P2P networks (digital social exchanges) on purchases (market exchanges); (3) the moderating effect of the felt personal relationship between consumers and interpreters on market exchanges; and (4) the fashion impact of music as a social identity indicator, irrespective of the way music is accessed.

2.1.1. Patterns of Accessing Music

Findings overall seem to be conditioned by different research designs, data and analyses. In spite of different motivations underpinning behaviour patterns, researchers have consistently found a pattern of heavy downloaders, occasional downloaders and purchasers. For a sample of 204 individuals, Molteni and Ordanini (2003) evaluated access to music through P2P networks, MP3 files and CDs based on six motivations. These authors identified five music consumer clusters: occasional downloaders (via MP3 sites), mass listeners (via P2P and MP3 sites), explorers/pioneers (mostly interested in searching for and exploring music), curious individuals (P2P site users, purely interested in entertainment) and duplicators (surfers of MP3 and P2P sites mainly for recording purposes). Walsh, Mitchell and Wiedmann (2003) studied 4,016 German music consumers mainly aged 20-39 years (70% of the sample), finding that 37% were regular downloaders of music from the Internet. These authors clustered — according to four latent motivations — music downloaders in three groups: demanding downloaders (motivated mainly by trend consciousness and topicality); general download approvers (motivated mainly by assortment and time advantage); and procurement autonomous downloaders (motivated mainly by independence).

2.1.2. The Impact of Digital Social Exchanges on Market Exchanges

This issue has been analysed indirectly through studies of the influences of downloading itself and of downloaded music volume as a proportion of all music. Al-Rafee and Cronan (2006) found, for a sample of 285 students, that subjective norms and happiness had a positive effect on downloading, while importance had a negative effect. For a sample of 4,460 Spaniards, Sandulli (2007) regressed a set of five factors (flexibility, discovery, community, assortment, and convenience) plus an index of the relative cost of CDs and P2P music on the proportion of P2P music accessed as compared to CDs owned (the lower the index, the higher the proportion of P2P music), then factored into the equation age, sex, willingness to pay, an indicator of having previously bought music online and the number of years using P2P. Sandulli (2007) found, in relation to P2P-owned music, that higher access proportions were associated with price, assortment and discovery, while lower proportions were associated with flexibility, age and willingness to pay. Their sample, it should be noted, was biased towards a younger age group of 18-24 year olds (74% of the sample). Like Al-Rafee and Cronan (2006), Chu and Lu (2007) studied the factors influencing online music purchase intentions for a data sample composed of 302 Taiwanese early adopters. They found that the perceived value of online music was a significant factor in predicting consumer online music purchase intentions, with this perception positively affected by usefulness and playfulness, and negatively affected by price and ease of use. Moreover, value perceptions differed, with actual purchasers affected positively by usefulness and negatively by price, and potential purchasers affected positively by playfulness and negatively by price (even more so than the purchasers).

2.1.3. The Moderating Effect of Felt Personal Relationships

Wang et al. (2009) and Ouellet (2007) analysed the impact of the consumer-interpreter relationship on music purchasing intentions. Wang et al. (2009) quantified this effect, labelled idolatry, for a sample of 350 teenagers in northern Taiwan, finding that downloading music had no significant bearing on the intention to buy music. The idolatry effect, even though it positively influenced purchase intentions, was lower for consumers with high download intentions. Ouellet (2007) found that preferences for particular music explained the need to acquire the music so as to be able to re-experience it (Lacher, 1989; Lacher & Mizerski, 1994), while attachment to performers — as with idolatry in the case of Wang et al. (2009) — explained the decision to purchase rather than download.

2.1.4. The Fashion Impact of Music as an Indicator of Social Identity

Chen, Shang and Lin (2008) used a representative stratified sample of 834 Taiwanese from Kuro (the biggest P2P community in Taiwan) to explore the background to music download intentions. Using three indicators of download intentions (fashion involvement, perceived value and perceived value difference) and a morality scale, they found that music was accessed through file sharing to maximize the consumption value. Interestingly, fashion involvement (an indicator of the social link between individuals in a group) affected both the intention to download and the perceived value of downloading. The authors conceptualized fashion involvement as an indicator of the degree to which individuals attempt to socially identify with members of a concrete social group by behaving like them (Miller, McIntyre & Mantrala, 1993; Reynolds, 1968; Sproles, 1979).

2.2. A Social Framework to Explain Music Access Patterns

Most research to date has explored individuals' motivations and their impact on the way they access music (particularly for downloading and purchases), whereas less attention has been paid to the social patterning of personal motivations and ways of accessing culture (see, e.g., Al-Rafee & Cronan, 2006; Chen et al., 2008; Chu & Lu, 2007; Molteni & Ordanini, 2003; Ouellet, 2007; Walsh et al., 2003). If social indicators were introduced in the analyses at all, they were used merely as control variables (Sandulli, 2007; Wang et al., 2009). However, these studies did report a significant correlation between social indicators and music acquisition practices. Wang et al. (2009), for instance, showed that age and being female were negatively correlated with the intention to buy; Sandulli (2007) — even though his sample was biased towards younger individuals — found that age was negatively associated with proportions of P2P music versus purchased CD music, with younger people possessing more downloaded music.

All this suggests that an individual's position in the social space is related to motivations and means regarding access to music. According to the theory of taste (Bourdieu, 1984), an individual's position in the social space is characterized by three properties, concretely: (1) their volume of capital; (2) the composition of the capital; and (3) the individual's trajectory in social space over time. Bourdieu suggests that the volume of capital and its composition are two principles of social differentiation, whereas an individual's social trajectory reveals how individuals transform their economic capital into cultural capital, and, in turn, their cultural capital into social capital — and, in so doing, change their position in social space over time. Bourdieu's theory of taste not only aims to explain taste in a particular temporal and spatial setting, but also how it varies with an individual's social position, emphasizing that individuals are, in fact, temporal occupants of social positions. His theory, then, suggests: (1) that social categories ought to be studied from a spatial and relational perspective that helps researchers uncover social structures for individual tastes and behaviours; and (2) that the interest in individuals resides in their trajectories in the social space. In this research we focused on Bourdieu's first proposition, as we were interested in how particular social categories are associated with access to music.

The structural view of the theory of taste suggests that positions in the social space are related to individual behaviours through the concept of *habitus*, which refers to a framework of interpretation and action that guides individuals when they make decisions about what to consume, how to access goods, how to consume them and how to interpret what others consume (Bourdieu, 1983, 1984, 1989). Bourdieu's relational view of social position has favoured the use of interdependence methods of analysis, particularly correspondence analysis. Interdependence methods propose that associations between social position indicators are due to unknown factors. It is these factors — Bourdieu's *habitus* — which relate the social space to the space of behaviours, motivations, preferences, and so on.

The *habitus*, which relates the social space to the space of interpretation and action, is a theoretical construct that goes beyond the concept of social class. For Bourdieu, social class is an empty construct — nothing more than the set of individuals that share a position in the social space as well as the *habitus* associated with those positions. Thus, its content changes as individuals occupying those positions change. A position in the social space, and its expected *habitus*, therefore, is not only defined through indicators of volume and variety of capital, but also through other social properties, such as gender, geographical location, ethnicity and age (Munk, 2003).

Most empirical work on the sociology of culture has researched whether individuals holding privileged positions have different musical genre tastes (Bourdieu, 1984; Peterson & Simkus, 1992; Peterson & Kern, 1996) and different patterns of attendance at cultural expressions (López-Sintas & García-Álvarez, 2004) and whether they even dine out differently (Warde, Martens & Olsen, 1999). According to Bourdieu's theory, preferences and actions are likely to be stratified, so differences in taste are interpreted as evidence in favour of Bourdieu's homology thesis (van Rees, Vermunt & Verboord, 1999). However, recent research findings suggest that individuals in privileged social positions show an omnivorous pattern of cultural consumption, favouring not only highbrow but also lowbrow or popular culture (Peterson & Simkus, 1992; Peterson & Kern, 1996; López-Sintas & García-Álvarez, 2004). This cultural omnivore thesis, however, has its critics (Bennett et al., 2005, 2008; Bennett, Savage, Silva, Warde, Gayo-Cal &

Wright 2009; Warde, Wright and Gayo-Cal, 2007), it being suggested that a boundary-effacement effect might be blurring the differentiation effect. However, if we approach differentiation, omnivorousness and boundary effacement not as competing, but as simultaneous, effects, we can measure their impact on individual behaviours and understand the social processes that simultaneously structure individual actions and interpretations (Holbrook, Weiss & Habich, 2002; López-Sintas & García-Álvarez, 2005).

Although how individual tastes are structured according to their capital has been widely researched (see Peterson, 2005), less attention has been paid to showing how other social categories influence taste or how individuals access and enjoy cultural expressions. Before the advent of the Internet, people typically purchased music and borrowed it from peers or from the local library. Internet has increased the possibilities for accessing cultural expressions (Nieckarz Jr., 2005; Verbood, 2010; Wikström, 2010); indeed, its influence on access to culture is so important that some researchers have suggested that the proposition "you are what you own" ought to be changed to "you are what you can access" (Belk, 2013). Research has largely focused on whether the Internet reduces or widens social differences, both in accessing culture and in other social categories that may play a role in structuring access to culture.

In the first case, researcher interest has centred on understanding the social categories associated with what is called the first digital divide, namely, access to the Internet (Riggins & Dewan, 2005; van Dijk, 2005). However, researchers soon noted that, irrespective of the issue of actual access to the Internet, online music access patterns depended on an individual's position in the social space (Kayahara & Wellman, 2007; Tepper & Hargittai, 2009; Tepper, Hargittai & Touve, 2007). This phenomenon came to be called the second digital divide (Attewell, 2001; Peter & Valkenburg, 2006; Rice & Katz, 2003) — a divide marked not so much by economic capital as by age, gender and cultural capital. Van Dijk (2006), generalizing the proposition of Douglas and Isherwood (1979), proposed that information in an information society becomes paramount in being able to function in and control society (2006:

page 231). However, cultural capital — a resource that is unequally distributed in society — is necessary to be able to select and process information.

Age, as an indicator of cultural tastes, has also revealed itself to be a structuring factor. Van Eijck (2001) researched the omnivore proposition for the Dutch population, finding that age structured music tastes. Older people tended to have highbrow tastes, whereas younger people — called the "new omnivores" by van Eijck (2001) — preferred pop/rock music. López-Sintas & García-Álvarez (2002a,2002b) and Coulangeon (2003) also found that age structured cultural tastes in the Spanish and French social spaces, respectively.

More recently, Tampubolon (2008a) used the US General Social Survey of 1993 to re-examine the relationship between social and cultural spaces, analysing musical genre data on likes and dislikes using methods for imputing missing values and a latent class model with multiple indicators and multiple independent causes. He found univorous and omnivorous patterns of music tastes (one and two in number, respectively), but his most striking finding was that the patterns were structured according to age and education and that age stratified tastes orthogonally to education. Purhonen, Gronow and Rahkonen (2009), in studying the music and literature likes and dislikes of the Finns, found that age, as well as gender, proved to be a structuring axis that was at least as important as education in explaining musical and literary tastes. Savage (2006) reported similar findings for research into musical genre likes and dislikes for a sample of British individuals. Therefore, if we take age as a social indicator of a life stage during which individuals develop music preferences — as suggested by Holbrook and Schindler (1994) and Bonneville-Roussy, Rentfrow, Xu and Potter (2013) — when we study access to music we should pay attention not only to Bourdieu's two principles of differentiation, but also to how an individual's life stage influences both their music preferences and the way they access culture.

To sum up, theory and evidence to date suggest that age and the economic and cultural capital of individuals are the two main factors structuring music tastes. We can thus expect that capital will influence how music is accessed, whereas age will influence music preferences and volume. Yet, to the best of our knowledge, no research has been performed that links music acquisition patterns to social position and life stage, or that explains these links. Here we provide a theoretical account and evidence regarding the social structuring of music access patterns. In particular, we examine the music access patterns for a sample of individuals and analyse associations between these patterns and (1) an individual's social position; (2) music buying and listening behaviour; and (3) reasons for downloading music.

3. Methodology

3.1. The Spanish Music Market

The Spanish music market has developed in a similar way to other national markets. From 2001, the sales value of music in traditional formats began to fall, dropping from 685 million euros to 257 million euros in 2007. This reduction occurred in parallel to a phenomenal rise in concert revenues for artists, which grew from 144 million euros in 2005 to 285 million euros in 2007 and 309 million euros in 2008. Record companies have thus started to impose what are called 360-degree contracts on artists that allow them to draw on all possible sources of income. Another watershed year in Spain was 2001, as Spanish artists were in a majority for the first time in the list of 50 best-selling albums, with the gap growing in the ensuing years (Promusicae, 2005: page 65). Contrasting with the fall in traditional sales, revenues from sales through mobile and online channels grew sixfold between 2004 and 2008, coming to represent 11% of total revenues in 2008. Although this rate of growth was faster than the world average, sales through these channels in Spain are still far from the 27% of industry revenues worldwide and the 40% for the US market (Fedea, 2010).

Access to the Internet in Spain (essential for online access to music) was 41% in 2008 (Fundación BBVA, 2008), a relatively low rate compared to other Western Europe countries, especially the Netherlands (87.8%). CDs are more expensive in Spain than in the USA or the rest of Europe (around double the price in the UK in absolute terms, for instance). Considering that average household income in the UK is almost double that of Spain, a CD in Spain is effectively around four times as expensive as in the UK.[1]

3.2. Data and Variables

The data for our study came from a Spanish survey on habits and cultural practices for 2006-2007 (for technical details, see Ministry of Culture, 2007). Surveyed were 14,822 Spanish and non-Spanish individuals of both sexes, aged 15 years and older, resident in Spain at the time of interview. The survey was conducted in four waves (one per quarter) between March 2006 and February 2007; each quarterly survey was based on a representative random sample of about 25% of the sampled individuals (all four quarterly surveys were used for our analysis), stratified by size according to autonomous community and municipality. This stratification by autonomous community was necessary to produce a representative sample with a 95% confidence level, not only at an aggregate level (age and gender) but also at the autonomous community level (Ministry of Culture, 2007).

In the interest of brevity, background data referring to the research described below are provided in supplementary form in Tables A1-A6.

3.2.1. Music Access Indicators

The volume of music accessed differed according to exchange type and format: for market exchanges, number of purchased albums/individual tracks; and for social exchanges, number of downloaded/copied albums/individual tracks. We thus established four music access indicators:

---

[1] See "Comprar música en España me cuesta el doble!" (Buying music in Spain costs double!), published in http://www.burbuja.info and "El precio de la cultura en España" (The price of culture in Spain), published in http://www.animaadversa.es.

purchased albums, purchased tracks, downloaded/copied albums and downloaded/copied tracks. The way music was bought or downloaded/copied was recorded through behaviour indicators (discussed below). As the four indicators did not follow a normal distribution, we split the original continuous variables into categorical variables: without activity, normal activity (1 to 10 units), and exceptional activity (more than 10 units). For convenience sake, the statistics for these variables are reported in the last column in Table 2 (discussed further below).

3.2.2. Social Space Indicators

According to Bourdieu's theoretical framework, the properties of individuals are indicators of their social position, such that variations in individual properties — level and structure of capital, age, gender, etc — are variations in the individual's social position that are, moreover, visible in a social map.

The Ministry of Culture survey on which we based our research elicited information on education as an indicator of cultural capital and on occupational status as an indicator of economic capital; however, it provided no occupational breakdown and nor did it collect information on incomes. As a proxy for economic capital in our study, therefore, we used occupational status,[2] namely, the following five categories: employed persons; entrepreneurs and self-employed workers (freelancers); unemployed persons; people receiving old-age or disability pensions and individuals performing unpaid domestic tasks (homemakers); and students. Educational attainment was recorded in three categories, as follows: third-level post-graduate education; third-level graduate education; and upper secondary education or below. Age, interpreted here as an indicator of an individual's life stage, was recorded in five categories. In order to complete the description of the social space, four additional variables were included, as follows: personal situation (five categories); number of individuals aged 15 and over in the household (three

---

2   The survey did not admit the possibility of allocation to social classes using, for instance, the Erikson–Goldthorpe–Portocarero class scheme (Erikson & Goldthorpe, 1992; Evans, 1992).

categories); habitat where the household was located (five categories); and sex (Table A1).

3.2.3. Music Consumption Motivations

Survey questions that analysed the social patterning of motivations behind music access decisions were as follows: reasons for buying copies of albums from fairs/street markets; reasons for downloading music free from the Internet; reasons for preferring free copies of albums; and reasons for not buying original albums (Table A2).

3.2.4. Behaviour Indicators

Given that music access patterns could possibly be interpreted in terms of an association with how frequently an individual listened to music, listening frequency was recorded for radio (daily, weekly, monthly, quarterly) and for any other device (daily, weekly, monthly, quarterly, yearly, rarely, never). Time dedicated to listening (hours) was recorded in terms of four categories: 0, 1-3 hours, 4-6 hours, and 7 or more hours weekly. (See the last column in Table A3 for the main statistics for the variables used in the analysis). To analyse purchase and download frequency, two nominal variables were used: date of last purchase (in the physical market or through the Internet), and date of last recording (copied from a CD, radio, TV or computer, or downloaded from the Internet for free). Respondents who bought or recorded music in the last quarter were asked to indicate where or how they acquired their last purchased album (original bought from a store, or original/copy bought from a fair/street market) or recorded album (copied from friends/family, or downloaded for free). Similar information was collected for individual tracks, for just two options: copied from friends/family, or downloaded for free (Table A3).

3.3. Analytical Procedure

We used an exploratory latent class model (Lazarsfeld & Henry, 1968), given that this consumer behaviour model uncovers consumption patterns for hedonic product categories (Boter & Wedel, 1999; Jedidi, Krider & Weinberg, 1998). To account for unobserved heterogeneity, the latent class model splits an original sample into T clusters or classes, so that the association between indicators is explained by probabilistic class membership. On the assumption that the association between music purchase and music downloading/copying indicators is due to unobserved heterogeneity in the population (in our case, classes of consumers of music), we investigated the proposition that access to music occurs in patterns.

To define our latent class model, we denoted as Y_1, Y_2, Y_3, and Y_4 the four indicators of music accessed through the market (purchased albums, purchased tracks, downloaded/copied albums, and downloaded/copied tracks). The entire set of indicators was denoted as **Y**. All the indicators were treated as ordered factors with three levels. The model estimated a set of parameters (cluster size and indicator probabilities conditioned to cluster membership) for the analysed population as follows:

$$P(\mathbf{Y}=\mathbf{y}) = \sum_{t=1}^{T} P(t) \prod_{i=1}^{4} P(Y_i = y_i | t).$$

Once the parameters were obtained, subsequent membership probabilities were calculated and each individual was exclusively assigned to a single cluster (Magidson & Vermunt, 2001). Note that the model did not include any social indicator as a predictor of class membership, as we wanted to subsequently check whether access patterns were socially structured (Le Roux & Rouanet, 2004). To estimate the cluster model we used LatentGold, version 4.0 (see Vermunt and Magidson, 2005).

Once individuals were clustered, we used social position indicators (age, occupational status, education and other social variables) and the other sets of explanatory indicators to describe the clusters, although note that these indicators did not participate in actually forming the behaviour clusters. The use of correspondence analysis to describe the set of clusters was a generalization of the usual ternary plots for when the number of clusters is greater than three (Magidson & Vermunt, 2001, 2004). To interpret the social space constructed in this way, we used the inertias (total variance) of the principal axes and the indicator contributions to the axes. Note that we used simple correspondence analysis as implemented by Nenadic and Greenacre (2007) in the R programming and data analysis environment (version 2.13, R Development Core Team, 2009) and, to test social music access patterns, we used the multinomial logit model implemented in SPSS 20.0.

4. Findings

4.1. Model Selection

Table 1 reports the statistics used to select the number of latent classes. The primary method for determining the number of latent classes is to statistically assess how latent class models fit the data using the likelihood ratio (L^2) statistic. Nevertheless, due to the sparseness of our data (more than 90% of individuals reported no activity for the indicators used), L^2 did not have an asymptotic chi-squared distribution and so could not be trusted for model selection using a statistical test. We therefore based our decision on heuristic methods, namely, two information criteria — the Bayesian information criterion (BIC) and the consistent Akaike information criterion (CAIC) (Fraley & Raftery, 1998; Raftery, 1986) — and the estimated proportion of classifications errors (see Vermunt & Magidson, 2005). Bearing in mind that lower values indicate a better model, Table 1 shows that the addition of the first two latent classes reduced L^2 by 81%; adding further latent classes (models with three to six classes) reduced the value of L^2 even further (by 9%, 3%, 1% and 1%, respectively). Both the BIC and CAIC indicated the best model to have four latent classes. The classification error hardly increased for the four-class model compared to the three-class model (both were within the limit proposed by van Rees et al. (1999), namely, 10%

of misclassifications); however, it did increase for the three-class and five-class models compared with the two-class and four-class models, respectively.[3]

Table 1. Goodness-of-fit statistics for the latent class models

Model	LL	Npar	L^2	BIC (L^2)	CAIC (L^2)	df	p-value	Class. err.
1-cluster	-22444.54	8	2600.8	1909.3	1837.2	72	1.8e-496	0.0000
2-cluster	-21387.62	13	486.9	-156.5	-223.5	67	5.1e-65	0.0681
3-cluster	-21270.23	18	252.1	-343.3	-405.3	62	9.1e-25	0.1043
4-cluster	-21227.28	23	166.2	-381.2	-438.2	57	1.3e-12	0.1088
5-cluster	-21210.05	28	131.8	-367.6	-419.6	52	7.3e-9	0.1793
6-cluster	-21196.91	33	105.5	-345.9	-392.9	47	2.2e-6	0.1749

4.2. Model Parameters

Table 2 shows the parameter estimates for the four-cluster model. The first row shows the proportion of individuals classified in each cluster, that is, $P(t)$, the relative size of the cluster. The next rows indicate behaviour probabilities given classification in a particular cluster, $P(Y = y_i|t)$. Thus, a respondent assigned to cluster one had an 87% probability of never buying an album, a 13% probability of buying fewer than ten albums a year and 0% probability of buying more than ten albums a year. The equivalent probabilities for a respondent assigned to cluster four were 3%, 86% and 11%, respectively.

---

[3] We estimated alternative models allowing some local dependencies between indicators with residuals higher than one, but they led to the same solution, although with more classification errors.

Table 2. Buying, copying and downloading probabilities (%)

	Cluster 1	Cluster 2	Cluster 3	Cluster 4	Sample
Cluster size, $P(t)$ (Std Err)	73.5% (0.02)	13% (0.01)	9% (0.01)	4.5% (0.02)	100%
Indicators, $P(y_i|t)$					
CDs: Volume purchased in the physical market and via the Internet (last 3 months)					
0	87% (0.02)	100% (0.02)	10% (0.04)	3% (0.02)	78.1%
1-10	13% (0.02)	0% (0.02)	86% (0.04)	86% (0.03)	21.1%
>10	0% (0.01)	0% (0.01)	4% (0.01)	11% (0.04)	0.8%
CDs: Volume downloaded/recorded/copied (last 3 months)					
0	98% (0.01)	38% (0.02)	42% (0.03)	100% (0.01)	85.8%
1-10	2% (0,01)	49% (.0.01)	47% (0.02)	0% (0.01)	11.6%
>10	0% (0.01)	13% (0.02)	11% (0.01)	0% (0,01)	2.7%
Tracks: Volume purchased via the Internet (last 3 months)					
0	100% (0.01)	100% (0.01)	95% (0.01)	89% (0.03)	99.0%
1-10	0% (0.01)	0% (0.01)	3% (0.01)	5% (0.01)	0.5%
>10	0% (0.01)	0% (0.01)	2% (0.01)	6% (0.02)	0.5%
Tracks: Volume downloaded/recorded/copied (last 3 months)					
0	99% (0.01)	49% (0.03)	60% (0.02)	97% (0.03)	89.2%
1-10	1% (0.01)	16% (0.01)	15% (0.01)	3% (0.02)	4.1%
>10	0% (0.01)	35% (0.02)	25% (0.02)	1% (0.01)	6.7%

The model suggested four clusters: one very large cluster (73.5% of the sample) of *non-accessers,* i.e., individuals who did not buy, download, or copy music, although they did listen to music (see below); a second cluster (13%) of *downloaders,* who downloaded most of their music free from P2P networks on the Internet; a third cluster (9%) of *copiers-buyers,* who had similar probabilities of buying albums and of copying albums/tracks from friends/family; and finally, a fourth cluster (4.5%) of *buyers*, with a very high probability of buying music, whether as an original or as a copy (from physical or online stores or from fairs/street markets). In the interest of brevity, the three clusters composed of downloaders, copiers-buyers and buyers will collectively be referred to below as "active" clusters. Note also that although the proportion of *non-accessers* may appear high, it is consistent with existing evidence regarding cultural participation (for a comprehensive review, see Peterson, 2005).

In interpreting the data regarding the four music access indicators (purchased albums, purchased tracks, downloaded/copied albums and downloaded/copied tracks), non-accessers were overrepresented in cluster one. *Downloaders* (cluster two) were overrepresented for downloading albums and tracks, but especially (more than fivefold) for the greatest activity level, i.e., downloading more than ten units. *Copiers-buyers* (cluster three) were overrepresented for all the higher activity levels for all four indicators (four- to sixfold and three- to fourfold when it came to buying and downloading/copying albums/tracks, respectively). Finally, *buyers* (cluster four) were only overrepresented for the higher activity levels for the purchasing indicators (almost 14 times and four- to eightfold for the highest and intermediate activity levels, respectively).

4.3. Social Position and Life Stage Indicators

The association between social space indictors and individuals classified in the four clusters is depicted in the symmetric correspondence analysis biplot shown in Figure 1, where the absolute contributions of points to axis variation are indicated by different colour intensities and where mass is indicated by size (see Nenadic & Greenacre, 2007). The first axis, which explained 93% of sample variation, orders clusters according to age, from younger (cluster two) to older (cluster one); the second axis, which explained 7% of sample variation, orders clusters two to four according to social position (from students and single individuals to individuals with the highest educational and occupational levels).

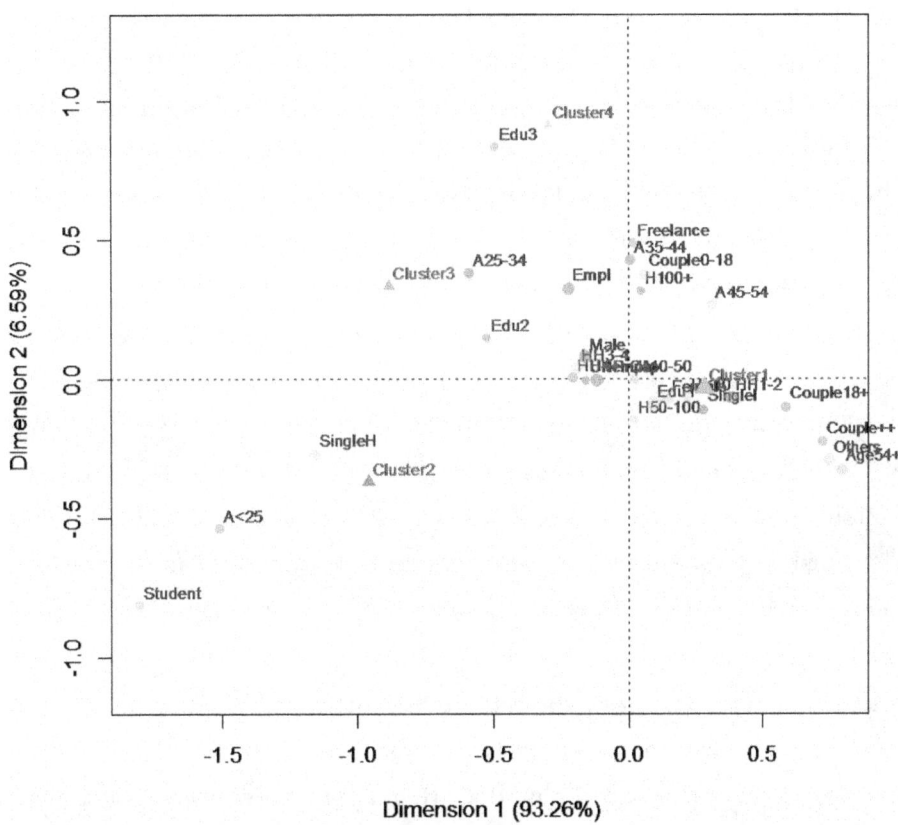

Figure 1. Clusters in the social space

Examining, in Figure 1, each of the profiles suggested by the four clusters in turn, *non-accessers* (cluster one) are typically women, aged 45 and older and with a basic education. They are overrepresented among homemakers and individuals receiving pensions, single independent individuals and couples with adult children, they are distributed among all habitat types except provincial capitals and they belong to households with two or fewer members. *Downloaders* (cluster two) are typically fairly well educated men, aged 25 or younger, single and living with their parents. They are either students or employed, live in provincial capitals or in cities of 50,000-100,000 inhabitants and tend to belong to larger households. *Copiers-buyers* (cluster three) are generally well positioned in the social hierarchy, being typically well educated men, aged under 34, generally self-employed or employed and either single and living with their parents or living in couples with young children. They tend to live in larger households in provincial capitals or in cities of above 100,000 inhabitants. Finally, *buyers* (cluster four) are also well positioned socially. They are mainly well educated, self-employed or employed men, aged under 54. They typically belong to larger households, live in couples with young children or are singles living with their parents and are resident in provincial capitals or cities above 100,000 inhabitants (Tables A1 and A4).

The motivations for acquiring music are depicted in Figure 2 (negative answers have been excluded to simplify the plot). The first axis, which explained 93% of sample variation, captures the gradient reflecting access to music through social exchanges, whether downloading or copying from friends/family. The second axis, which explained the remaining 7% of sample variation, orders clusters two to four according to motivations to access music from fairs/street markets (mainly *buyers* and, to a lesser extent, *copiers-buyers*).

Non-accessers and *buyers* showed little motivation to download music. In fact, simple correspondence analysis located these clusters near each other and far from the other two clusters. Regarding these latter two clusters, certain reasons for copying (less expensive and faster) or downloading (more convenient, less expensive, and more immediate) were more important for *downloaders* than for *copiers-buyers*. Moreover, *downloaders* acquired tracks as well as albums and the possibility of downloading from the Internet was, in fact, a reason for not buying more original albums (Tables A2 and A5).

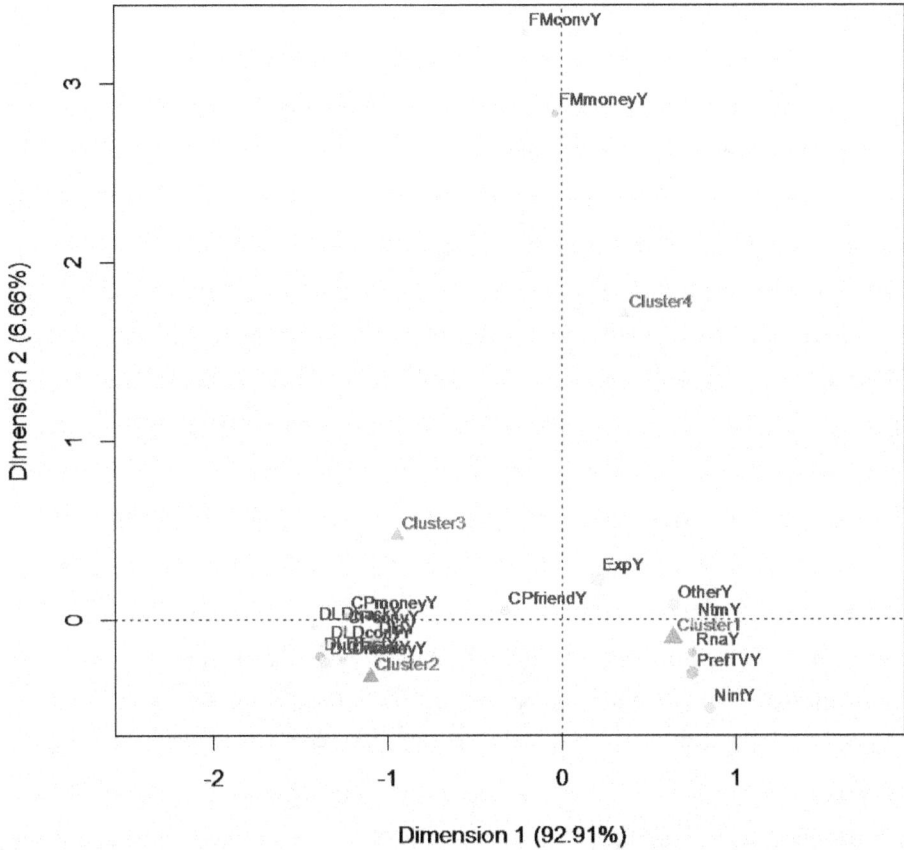

Figure 2. Clusters in the motivation space

The actual temporal pattern of accessing and listening music is depicted in Figure 3 (as with Figure 2, negative answers have been excluded to simplify the plot). According to the contributions of points to axes and axes to points (see absolute and relative contributions, respectively, in Table A6), the first axis, which explained 70% of sample variation, captures the gradient referring to access to music. To the left — where the cluster of *non-accessers* is located — are responses reflecting low music listening frequency; to the right are responses reflecting high music listening frequency. The second axis, which explained the other 30% of sample variation, orders individuals from the three active clusters according to how they accessed music, whether as *downloaders* (cluster two) or as *buyers* (mainly cluster four and, to a lesser extent, cluster three).

Non-accessers (cluster one) were overrepresented for all indicators reflecting low listening, recording and purchasing frequencies. They were overrepresented for radio listening frequency (at least once quarterly, followed by at least once monthly and once weekly) and, likewise, for listening via music players (never, at least once a year or less often than once a year). As for recording, *non-accessers* either never recorded music or, if they did so, it was a long time ago (more than one to two years ago). Finally, they never bought music (albums or tracks) through any distribution channel or, if they had, their last purchase was typically last year or more than a year previously (Table A3).

Downloaders (cluster two) were more frequent radio music listeners, with individuals who listened frequently to music players (every day or every week) especially overrepresented. Like the *non-accessers*, they were not interested in buying music, as indicated by the fact that their last purchase was a year or more ago; however, they did record music frequently (they typically did so in the last three months), showing a preference for free albums or tracks (the Internet and, to a lesser degree, copies from friends/family).

As for clusters three and four, *buyers* dedicated quite a lot of time to listening to music, doing so daily irrespective of the device. They infrequently recorded music, as indicated by the fact that their most recent recording (if any) dated from the previous year or further back in time. They generally purchased music, being overrepresented in terms of purchases in the last quarter, mainly from stores and fairs/street markets (both originals and copies from the latter). As would be expected, *copiers-buyers* occupied the space between *downloaders* and *buyers*, with similar behaviour regarding music listening frequency (any device) and the time allotted to music weekly. The main difference between *copiers-buyers* and the other active clusters was in the consumption of free music (very similar to *downloaders*) and purchased music (very similar to *buyers*).

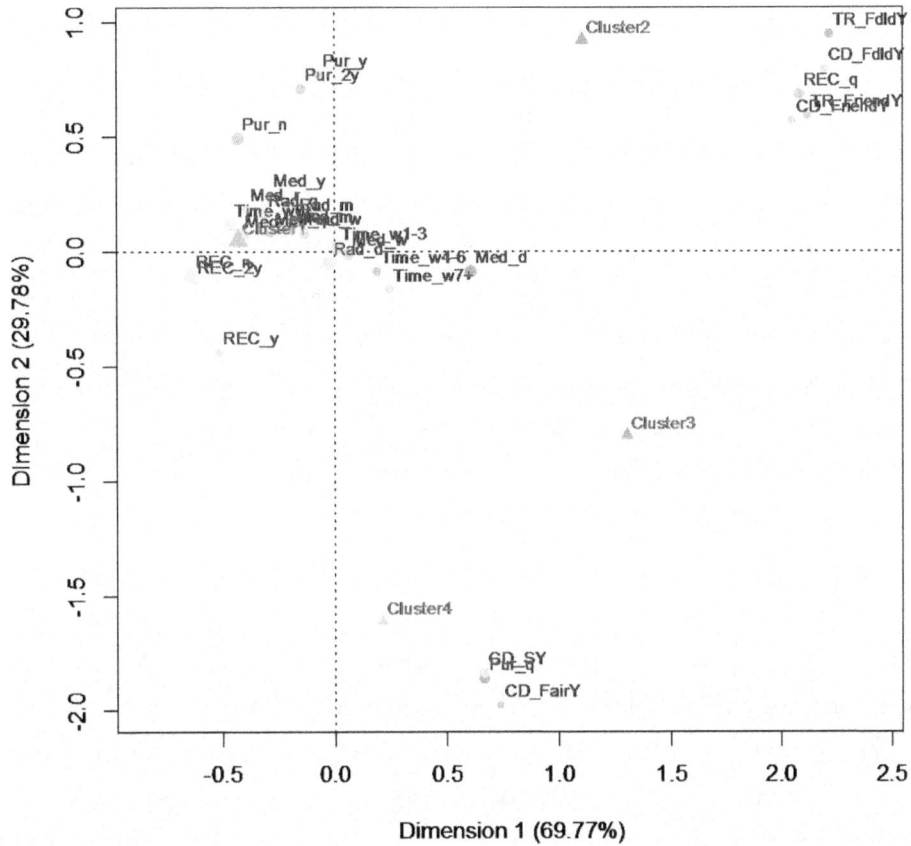

Figure 3. Clusters in the behaviour space

5. Discussion

The theoretical framework developed above suggests that music access patterns and the volume of music accessed are both socially structured. Our findings indicate that this is actually the case. We identified four music consumer profiles: individuals who did not buy, download or copy music (cluster one, 73.5%); individuals who almost exclusively downloaded music for free from P2P networks (cluster two, 13%); individuals who were equally likely to purchase music or copy it from friends/family (cluster three, 9%); and individuals who mainly bought music (cluster four, 4.5%). This pattern, as well as corroborating the evidence provided by Molteni and Ordanini (2003) and Walsh et al. (2003), also introduces a social dimension to the interpretation of how and why people access music.

Our findings, reflecting those reported by Tampubolon (2008a), suggest that music access is structured by life stage and by position in the social space in terms of both economic and cultural capital. Age and education, in particular, have been demonstrated to be independent of each other in how they affect the way people access music. The first axis in our Figure 1, associated with age, orders music access patterns from *downloaders* (younger individuals) to *non-accessers* (older individuals); the second axis, associated with education, orders access patterns from *downloaders* (less well educated) to *buyers* (better educated). These findings reflect those reported by López-Sintas, García-Álvarez and Filimon (2008) and Tampubolon (2008a).

The same patterns are reproduced, to a statistically significant degree, in a multinomial logit model, suggesting that both this model and the correspondence analysis produce equivalent results. Correspondence analysis, however, is better equipped to deal with the interdependence between indicators of social position, which, by definition, must be correlated, whereas generalized linear models perform better than interdependence models when independent indicators are not correlated. This argument explains Bourdieu's preference for interdependence models, and particularly for correspondence analysis (Bourdieu, Chamboredon & Passeron 1991). Nonetheless, the findings provided by both models furnish evidence in the same direction, with both suggesting that the age gradient is orthogonal to the education gradient in regard to ways of accessing music. Even though our data do not allow us to explore whether individuals first turn to their social networks to obtain information and later access the corresponding cultural expressions on the Internet (as reported in Kayahara & Wellman, 2007; Tepper & Hargittai, 2009), our findings agree with those of Tepper and Hargittai (2009), who reported that individuals with different education levels have different patterns of music access.

Coulangeon (2003), López-Sintas and García-Álvarez (2002a, 2002b), Savage (2006), Tampubolon (2006, 2008a) and van Eijck (2001) already noted this pattern concerning music tastes but did not provide any theoretical explanation. According to our framework, the reason age — as an indicator of life stage — structures music access is because young individuals need to access large volumes of music, irrespective of their social position (see Bonneville-Roussy et al., 2013). Position in the social space, meanwhile, as reflected by education, structures the means used by individuals to access music (López-Sintas et al., 2008; Tampubolon, 2008a). Bonneville-Roussy et al. (2013) suggest that the importance attributed to music declines with age, with young people listening to music significantly more often than middle-aged adults; they also reported that while people, as they age, listen less to music, if they do listen, it is mainly to the music of their youth (see Holbrook & Schindler, 1994). These propositions are entirely coherent with our findings in the research described above.

Our findings enable us to interpret evidence provided by Sandulli (2007) in regard to the fact that the ratio of downloaded to purchased music fell as age increased; thus, older and wealthier individuals possessed more albums but probably also had stopped acquiring music. In fact, how individuals access music seems to follow the clockwise trajectory depicted in Figure 4: they start out as *downloaders*, then become *copiers-buyers*, then become *buyers* and close the circle as *non-accessers*. Although this proposition cannot be tested with our data, it can be inferred from the findings of Bonneville-Roussy et al. (2013). Additionally, according to Ouellet (2007) and Wang et al. (2009), acquiring from any source does not affect music buying behaviour, but attachment to performers has a positive impact on the intention to buy music. For *downloaders*, therefore, the Internet is simply a rapid and more convenient means of accessing music that hardly affects their intention to buy.

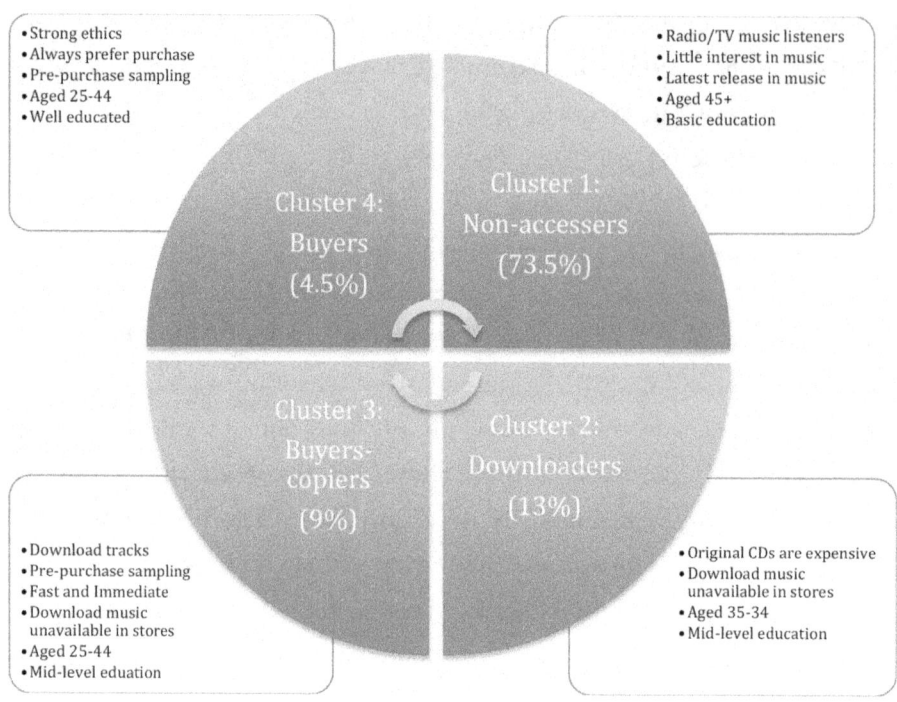

Figure 4. Clockwise model of access to music

There thus seem to be two forces that structure music access: a positive one between age and purchase (an inverted U), and a negative one between age and volume (of either downloaded/copied or purchased music). This pattern is coherent with the explanation of musical taste formation — as proposed by Holbrook and Schindler (1994) — in the 16-26 age bracket, when people acquire and consume most music. Note, however, that this finding regarding age is somewhat conditioned by both sex and socioeconomic status. Consistent with those earlier conclusions regarding age, our findings can be interpreted as confirming that younger consumers download music (or buy it when they can afford it), whereas individuals aged 54 and older acquire little, if any, music (by any means) because — following Holbrook and Schindler (1994) — they simply prefer to re-experience the music of their youth. North and Oishi (2006) reported similar findings.

Regarding limitations to our findings, our analysis relied on a cross-sectional sample, not panel data, so it was not possible to disentangle age, cohort and period effects — as was done, for instance, by Peterson and Kern (1996) for their study of highbrow taste. Although it is indeed true that people's familiarity with digital technological devices is affected by both a strong age gradient and generational bias, our aim was to describe how younger individuals access more music than their elders —independently of social position and cohort differences — and explain why and how music access is socially structured. Our findings broadly suggest that as people age, they gradually access less music and also change the way they access music. We were unable to study generational differences in volume of music accessed nor could we compare — as Peterson and Kern (1996) did — whether cohorts of the same age in different generations (20 years apart) accessed greater or lesser volumes of music.

6. Conclusions

We furnish a structural social interpretation of music access patterns, based on an individual's position in the social space as reflected by indicators of their capital and life stage. A position in the social space, and its expected *habitus*, is not only defined by indicators of volume and variety of capital, but also by other social categories. According to our evidence, and as suggested by our proposed theory, music access and listening patterns are both structured by an individual's social position (indicated by education) and life stage (indicated by age). Our findings reveal that the social framework we have constructed: (1) explains why music access is socially structured by (at least) two independent gradients, namely, life stage and social position; and (2) potentially interprets unexpected findings reported by research framed in an individualistic framework.

J. López-Sintas, À. Cebollada-Frontera, N. Filimon, A. Ghahraman

Acknowledgments

This research has been possible thanks to funding from the Centre d'Estudis i de Recerca d'Humanitats (CERHUM) at the Universitat Autònoma de Barcelona, the European Union ERDF Programme and the Spanish Ministry of Education and Science (Research Project ECO2011-29558-C02-01-E) and the Catalan Autonomous Government/Agència de Gestió d'Ajuts Universitaris i de Recerca (AGAUR) (Grant 2014-SGR-502). We would also like to thank the Spanish Ministry of Culture for kindly providing the data used for this research.

References

Al-Rafee, S., & Cronan, T.P. (2006). Digital piracy: factors that influence attitude toward behaviour. *Journal of Business Ethics,* 63, 237-259.
http://dx.doi.org/10.1007/s10551-005-1902-9

Attewell, P. (2001). Comment: The First and Second Digital Divides. *Sociology of Education,* 74(3), 252-259.
http://dx.doi.org/10.2307/2673277

Belk, R.W. (2013). Extended Self in a Digital World. *Journal of Consumer Research* 40(3), 477-500.
http://dx.doi.org/10.1086/671052

Bennett, T., Emmisson, M., & Frow, J. (1999). *Accounting for tastes. Australian everyday cultures.* Cambridge: Cambridge University Press.

Bennett, T., Savage, M., Silva, E.B., Warde, A., Gayo-Cal, M., & Wright, D. (2005). *Cultural capital and the cultural field in contemporary Britain.* Manchester, UK.

Bennett, T., Savage, M., Silva, E.B., Warde, A., Gayo-Cal, M., & Wright, D. (2008). *Culture, Class, Distinction.* Taylor & Francis. Retrieved from http://books.google.com.au/books?id=UJGNwyWXqlUC

Bennett, T., Savage, M., Silva, E.B., Warde, A., Gayo-Cal, M., & Wright, D. (2009). *Culture, Class, Distinction* (1st edition). New York: Routledge.

Bonneville-Roussy, A., Rentfrow, P.J., Xu, M.K., & Potter, J. (2013). Music through the ages: Trends in musical engagement and preferences from adolescence through middle adulthood. *Journal of Personality and Social Psychology,* 105(4), 703-717.
http://dx.doi.org/10.1037/a0033770

Boter, J., & Wedel, M. (1999). Segmentation of hedonic consumption: an application of latent class analysis to consumer transaction databases. *Journal of Market-Focused Management*, 3(3/4), 295-311.
http://dx.doi.org/10.1023/A:1009855123617

Bourdieu, P. (1983). Forms of capital. In Richardson, J.G. (Ed.). *Handbook of theory and research for the sociology of education*. Westport, CT: Greenwood. 241-258.

Bourdieu, P. (1984). *Distinction: a social critique of the judgment of taste*. London: Routledge.

Bourdieu, P. (1989). *Outline of a theory of practice*. Cambridge: Cambridge University Press.

Bourdieu, P., Chamboredon, J.C., & Passeron, J.C. (1991). *The Craft of Sociology*. Berlin: Walter de Guyter.
http://dx.doi.org/10.1515/9783110856460

Chen, Y.C., Shang, R.A., & Lin, A.K. (2008). The intention to download music files in a P2P environment: consumption value, fashion and ethical decision perspectives. *Electronic Consumer Research and Applications*, 7, 411-422.
http://dx.doi.org/10.1016/j.elerap.2008.02.001

Chu, C.W., & Lu, H.P. (2007). Factors influencing online music purchase intention in Taiwan. An empirical study based on the value-intention framework. *Internet Research*, 17(2), 139-155.
http://dx.doi.org/10.1108/10662240710737004

Coulangeon, P. (2003). La stratification sociale des goûts musicaux: le modèle de la légitimité culturelle en question. *Revue Française de Sociologie*, 44(1), 3-33.
http://dx.doi.org/10.3917/rfs.441.0003

Douglas, M., & Isherwood, B. (1979). *The world of goods*. London: Routledge.

Erikson, R., & Goldthorpe, J.H. (1992). *The constant flux: a study of class mobility in industrial societies*. Oxford: Calendon Press.

Evans, G. (1992). Testing the validity of the Goldthorpe class schema. *European Sociological Review*, 8, 211-232.

Fedea (2010). *Informe sobre la industria de la música*. Madrid: Fedea.

Fraley, C., & Raftery, A.E. (1998). How many clusters? Which clustering methods? Answers via model-based cluster analysis. *Computer Journal*, 41, 578-588.
http://dx.doi.org/10.1093/comjnl/41.8.578

Fundación BBVA (2008). *Internet en España*. Bilbao, Spain: Departamento de Estudios Sociales, Fundacón BBVA.
http://www.fbbva.es/TLFU/dat/Estudio_Internet_2008.pdf

Holbrook, M.B., & Schindler, R.M. (1994). Age, sex and attitude toward the past as predictors of consumers' aesthetic tastes for cultural products. *Journal of Marketing Research*, 31(August), 412-422.
http://dx.doi.org/10.2307/3152228

Holbrook, M.B., Weiss, M.J., & Habich, J. (2002). Disentangling Effacement, Omnivore and Distinction Effects on the Consumption of Cultural Activities: An Illustration. *Marketing Letters,* 13(4), 345-357.
http://dx.doi.org/10.1023/A:1020322600709

Jedidi, K., Krider, R.E., & Weinberg, C.B. (1998). Clustering at the movies. *Marketing Letters,* 9(4), 393-405.
http://dx.doi.org/10.1023/A:1008097702571

Kayahara, J., & Wellman, B. (2007). Searching for culture—high and low. *Journal of Computer-Mediated Communication,* 12(3), Art. 4.
http://dx.doi.org/10.1111/j.1083-6101.2007.00352.x

Lacher, K.T. (1989). Hedonic consumption: music as a product. In Srull, T.K., & Provo, U.T. (Ed.). *Advances in Consumer Research,* 16. Minnesota: Association for Consumer Research. 367-373.

Lacher, K.T., & Mizerski, R. (1994). An exploratory study of the responses and relationships involved in the evaluation of and in the intention to purchase new rock music. *Journal of Consumer Research,* 21, 366-380.
http://dx.doi.org/10.1086/209404

Lazarsfeld, P.F., & Henry, N.W. (1968). *Latent structure analysis.* Boston: Houghton Mifflin.

Le Roux, B., & Rouanet, H. (2004). *Geometric Data Analysis.*
http://dx.doi.org/10.1007/1-4020-2236-0

Liebowitz, S.J. (2005). Pitfalls in measuring the impact of file-sharing on the sound recording market. *CESifo Economic Studies,* 51(2-3), 435-473.
http://dx.doi.org/10.1093/cesifo/51.2-3.435

Liebowitz, S.J., & Watt, R. (2006). How to best ensure remuneration for creators in the market for music? Copyright and its alternatives. *Journal of Economic Surveys,* 20(4), 513-545.
http://dx.doi.org/10.1111/j.1467-6419.2006.00259.x

López-Sintas, J., & García-Álvarez, E. (2002a). Omnivores show up again: the segmentation of cultural consumers in Spanish social space. *European Sociological Review,* 18(3), 353-368.
http://dx.doi.org/10.1093/esr/18.3.353

López-Sintas, J., & García-Álvarez, E. (2002b). The consumption of cultural products: an analysis of the Spanish social space. *Journal of Cultural Economics,* 26(2), 115-138.
http://dx.doi.org/10.1023/A:1014473618476

López-Sintas, J., García-Álvarez, E., & Filimon, N. (2008). Scale and periodicities of consuming recorded music: reconciling Bourdieu's theory of taste with facts. *The Sociological Review,* 56(1), 78-101.
http://dx.doi.org/10.1111/j.1467-954X.2008.00778.x

López-Sintas, J., & García-Álvarez, E. (2004). Omnivore versus univore consumption and its symbolic properties: evidence from Spaniards' performing arts attendance. *Poetics*, 32, 463-483.

López-Sintas, J., & García-Álvarez, E. (2005). Four characters on the stage playing three games: performing arts consumption in Spain. *Journal of Business Research* 58(10), 1446-1455.
http://dx.doi.org/10.1016/j.jbusres.2003.10.013

Magidson, J., & Vermunt, J.K. (2001). Latent class factor and cluster models, bi-plots and related graphical displays. In Sober, M., & Becker, M. (Eds.). *Sociological Methodology*, 31. Boston: Blackwell. 223-264.
http://dx.doi.org/10.1111/0081-1750.00096

Magidson, J., & Vermunt, J.K. (2004). Latent Class Models. In Kaplan, D. (Ed.). *Handbook for Quantitative Methodology*. Thousand Oaks, CA: Sage. 175-198.
http://dx.doi.org/10.4135/9781412986311.n10

Ministry of Culture (Spain) (2007). Encuesta de hábitos y practicas culturales 2006-2007.
http://www.mcu.es/estadisticas/MC/EHC/2006/Presentacion.html

Michel, N.J. (2004). *Internet file sharing: the evidence so far and what it means for the future*. The Heritage Foundation.
http://www.heritage.org/Research/InternetandTechnology/bg1790.cfm

Miller, C.M., McIntyre, S.H., & Mantrala, M.K. (1993). Toward formalizing fashion theory. *Journal of Marketing Research*, 30(2), 142-157.
http://dx.doi.org/10.2307/3172824

Molteni, L., & Ordanini, A. (2003). Consumption patterns, digital technology and music downloading. *Long Range Planning*, 36, 389-406.
http://dx.doi.org/10.1016/S0024-6301(03)00073-6

Munk, M.D. (2003). *The trace of social space — the theory of strategies of reconversions*. Danish National Institute of Social Research, Copenhagen, Denmark.
http://www.skeptron.uu.se/broady/sec/p-munk-traces-030116.pdf

Nenadic, O., & Greenacre, M. (2007). Correspondence Analysis in R, with Two- and Three-dimensional Graphics: The ca Package. *Journal of Statistical Software*, 20(3), 1-13.

Nieckarz Jr., P.P. (2005). Community in Cyber Space? The Role of the Internet in Facilitating and Maintaining a Community of Live Music Collecting and Trading. *City and Community*, 4(4), 403-423.
http://dx.doi.org/10.1111/j.1540-6040.2005.00145.x

North, A.C., & Oishi, A. (2006). Music CD purchase decisions. *Journal of Applied Social Psychology*, 36(12), 3043-3084.
http://dx.doi.org/10.1111/j.0021-9029.2006.00142.x

Ouellet, J.F. (2007). The purchase versus illegal download of music by consumers: the influence of consumer response towards the artist and music. *Canadian Journal of Administrative Sciences*, 24, 107-119.
http://dx.doi.org/10.1002/cjas.16

Peter, J., & Valkenburg, P.M. (2006). Adolescents' Internet use: Testing the "disappearing digital divide" versus the "emerging digital differentiation" approach. *Poetics*, 34(4-5), 293-305.
http://dx.doi.org/10.1016/j.poetic.2006.05.005

Peterson, R.A. (2005). Problems in comparative research: the example of omnivorousness. *Poetics*, 33, 257-282.
http://dx.doi.org/10.1016/j.poetic.2005.10.002

Peterson, R.A., & Kern, R.M. (1996). Changing Highbrow Taste: From Snob to Omnivore. *American Sociological Review*, 61(October), 900-907.
http://dx.doi.org/10.2307/2096460

Peterson, R.A., & Simkus, A. (1992). How musical tastes mark occupational status groups. In Lamont, M., & Fournier, M. (Eds.). *Cultivating Differences*. Chicago: University of Chicago Press. 152-186.

Promusicae (2005). *El libro blando de la música en España*. Madrid: Promusicae.

Purhonen, S., Gronow, J., & Rahkonen, K. (2009). Social differentiation of musical and literary taste patterns in Finland. *Research on Finnish Society*, 2, 39-49.

R Development Core Team (2009). R: A language and environment for statistical computing. R Foundation for Statistical Computing, Vienna, Austria.
http://www.r-project.org/

Raftery, A.E. (1986). Choosing models for cross-classifications. *American Sociological Review*, 51, 145-146.
http://dx.doi.org/10.2307/2095483

Reynolds, W.H. (1968). Cars and clothing: understanding fashion trends. *Journal of Marketing*, 32(7), 44-49.
http://dx.doi.org/10.2307/1249761

Rice, R.E., & Katz, J.E. (2003). Comparing internet and mobile phone usage: digital divides of usage, adoption and dropouts. *Telecommunications Policy*, 27(8-9), 597-623.
http://dx.doi.org/10.1016/S0308-5961(03)00068-5

Riggins, F., & Dewan, S. (2005). The Digital Divide: Current and Future Research Directions. *Journal of the Association for Information Systems*, 6(12).
http://aisel.aisnet.org/jais/vol6/iss12/13

Sandulli, F.D. (2007). CD music purchase behaviour of P2P users. *Technovation*, 27, 325-334.
http://dx.doi.org/10.1016/j.technovation.2006.12.007

Savage, M. (2006). The musical field. *Cultural Trends*, 15(2-3), 159-174.
http://dx.doi.org/10.1080/09548960600712975

Sproles, G.B. (1979). *Fashion: consumer behavior toward dress.* Minneapolis: Burgess Publishing.

Tampubolon, G. (2006). *The problem of variety and symbolic boundary in cultural tastes.* CRESC. Mimeographed.

Tampubolon, G. (2008a). Revisiting omnivores in America circa 1990s: The exclusiveness of omnivores? *Poetics,* 36(2-3), 243-264.
http://dx.doi.org/10.1016/j.poetic.2008.02.007

Tepper, S.J., & Hargittai, E. (2009). Pathways to music exploration in a digital age. *Poetics,* 37(3), 227-249.
http://dx.doi.org/10.1016/j.poetic.2009.03.003

Tepper, S.J., Hargittai, E., & Touve, D. (2007). Music, Mavens and Technology. In Tepper, S.J., & Ivey, B. (Eds.). *Engaging Art: The Next Great Transformation of America's Cultural Life* (1st edition). London: Routledge. 199-220.

Van Dijk, J.A.G.M. (2005). *The Deepening Divide: Inequality in the Information Society.* Thousand Oaks, CA: Sage.

Van Dijk, J.A.G.M. (2006). Digital divide research, achievements and shortcomings. *Poetics,* 34(4-5), 221-235.
http://dx.doi.org/10.1016/j.poetic.2006.05.004

Van Eijck, K. (2001). Social differentiation in musical taste patterns. *Social Forces,* 79(3), 1163-1184.
http://dx.doi.org/10.1353/sof.2001.0017

Van Rees, K., Vermunt J., & Verboord, M. (1999). Cultural classifications under discussion. Latent class analysis of highbrow and lowbrow reading. *Poetics,* 26, 349-365.
http://dx.doi.org/10.1016/S0304-422X(99)00019-4

Verboord, M. (2010). The Legitimacy of Book Critics in the Age of the Internet and Omnivorousness: Expert Critics, Internet Critics and Peer Critics in Flanders and the Netherlands. *European Sociological Review,* 26(6), 623-637.
http://dx.doi.org/10.1093/esr/jcp039

Vermunt, J.K., & Magidson, J. (2005). *LatentGold4.0: User's Guide.* Belmunt, MA: Statistical Innovations.

Walsh, G., Mitchell, V.W., & Wiedmann, K.P. (2003). Internet-induced changes in consumer music procurement behaviour: a German perspective. *Marketing Intelligence and Planning,* 21(5), 305-317.
http://dx.doi.org/10.1108/02634500310490256

Wang, C., Chen, C., Yang, S., & Farn, C. (2009). Pirate or buy? The moderating effect of idolatry. *Journal of Business Ethics,* 90(1), 81-93.
http://dx.doi.org/10.1007/s10551-009-0027-y

Warde, A., Martens, L., & Olsen, W. (1999). Consumption and the problem of variety: cultural omnivorousness, social distinction and dining out. *Sociology,* 33(1), 105-127.
http://dx.doi.org/10.1177/S0038038599000061

Warde, A., Wright, D., & Gayo-Cal, M. (2007). Understanding Cultural Omnivorousness: Or, the Myth of the Cultural Omnivore. *Cultural Sociology*, 1(2), 143-164.
http://dx.doi.org/10.1177/1749975507078185

Williams, J.P. (2006). Authentic Identities. *Journal of Contemporary Ethnography*, 35(2), 173-200.

Wikström, P. (2010). The Music Industry: Music in the Cloud (1st edition). Cambridge; Malden, MA: Polity.

Annex

Table A1. Sociodemographic characteristics (row profiles in %)

Clusters	1	2	3	4	Sample
Overall	73.5%	13%	9%	4.5%	100%
Occupational status					
Self-employed *(Freelance)*	73%	10%	10%	7%	9%
Employed *(Empl)*	69%	14%	11%	6%	41%
Unemployed *(Unempl)*	71%	15%	9%	5%	6%
Homemaker, retired, with disability *(Others)*	91%	5%	2%	2%	35%
Student *(Student)*	38%	38%	20%	4%	9%
Personal situation					
Single, living w/parents *(SingleH)*	51%	28%	17%	5%	22%
Single/divorced/widowed/separated, no dependent children *(SingleI)*	80%	10%	6%	4%	13%
Couple w/children <18 at home *(Couple0-18)*	75%	10%	9%	6%	34%
Couple w/children ≥18 at home *(Couple18+)*	87%	6%	4%	3%	16%
Couple w/children ≥18 not at home and other *(Couple++)*	90%	5%	2%	3%	15%
Habitat (thousands)					
Provincial capital *(HPrCap)*	72%	14%	9%	5%	43%
>100 *(H100+)*	74%	10%	10%	5%	8%
50-100 *(H50-100)*	75%	14%	7%	4%	7%
10-50 *(H10-50)*	75%	12%	9%	4%	23%
<10 *(H<10)*	79%	10%	7%	4%	19%

Clusters	1	2	3	4	Sample
Household size (persons >15 years)					
2 or fewer *(HH1-2)*	**82%**	8%	6%	4%	33%
3-4 *(HH3-4)*	70%	**15%**	**10%**	**5%**	53%
> 4 *(HH4+)*	70%	**15%**	**10%**	**5%**	14%
Age (years)					
< 25 *(A<25)*	44%	**33%**	**19%**	4%	14%
25-34 *(A25-34)*	61%	**18%**	**15%**	**7%**	17%
35-44 *(A35-44)*	73%	11%	**10%**	**6%**	19%
45-54 *(A45-54)*	**80%**	8%	7%	**5%**	16%
>54 *(A54+)*	**92%**	4%	2%	2%	34%
Sex					
Female *(Female)*	**77%**	11%	7%	4%	52%
Male *(Male)*	71%	**14%**	**10%**	**5%**	48%
Education					
Upper secondary or below *(Edu1)*	**76%**	12%	8%	4%	85%
Third-level graduate *(Edu2)*	63%	**18%**	**13%**	**6%**	7%
Third-level post-graduate *(Edu3)*	62%	**15%**	**14%**	**9%**	8%

Overrepresented indicators in bold.

Variables (labels for graphed variables in italics).

Note: The first row of this table shows the proportion of individuals classified in each cluster, that is, $P(t)$, the relative size of the cluster. The next rows describe the profile of each cluster according to the users' descriptors. That is, given that an individual is self-employed, $P(T=t|y_i)$, its probability of being classified in cluster one is 73%, in cluster one, 10%, and so on. The following tables describe clusters according to individuals' motivations and behaviours.

Table A2. *Music consumption motivations (row profiles in %)*

Clusters	1	2	3	4	Sample
Overall	73.5%	13%	9%	4.5%	100%
Reasons for buying copied albums from fairs/street markets (FM)					
Convenient Yes *(FMconvY)*	32%	0%	45%	23%	1%
Money savings Yes *(FMmoneyY)*	41%	0%	38%	21%	2%
Reasons for downloading for free (DLD)					
Convenient Yes *(DLDconvY)*	9%	57%	33%	1%	8%
Fast and immediate Yes *(DLDfastY)*	8%	60%	32%	1%	5%
Money savings Yes *(DLDmoneyY)*	9%	59%	31%	1%	10%
Only one track wanted Yes *(DLDtrackY)*	6%	58%	35%	1%	2%
Reasons for preferring free copies (CP)					
Convenient Yes *(CPconvY)*	13%	52%	34%	1%	2%
Fast and immediate Yes *(CPfastY)*	13%	56%	31%	0%	1%
Money savings Yes *(CPmoneyY)*	13%	51%	35%	1%	3%

Clusters	1	2	3	4	Sample
Reasons for NOT buying originals					
Copy from friends/family Yes *(CPfriendY)*	46%	**30%**	**20%**	3%	7%
Download Yes *(DldY)*	19%	**52%**	**27%**	2%	9%
Expensive Yes *(ExpY)*	65%	17%	12%	**6%**	50%
Latest release not available Yes *(RnaY)*	**88%**	5%	4%	3%	5%
Little interest in music Yes *(NintY)*	**94%**	4%	1%	1%	11%
No time Yes *(NtmY)*	**87%**	4%	4%	5%	6%
Prefer radio/TV Yes *(PrefTVY)*	**89%**	5%	3%	3%	23%
Other reasons Yes *(OtherY)*	**82%**	6%	6%	**5%**	16%

Overrepresented indicators in bold.

Variables (labels for graphed variables in italics).

Table A3. Behaviour patterns (row profiles in %)

Clusters	1	2	3	4	Sample
Overall	73.5%	13%	9%	4.5%	100%
Frequency of listening to radio-broadcast music					
Every day (Rad_d)	71%	13%	**10%**	**6%**	55%
Every week (Rad_w)	**75%**	13%	8%	4%	16%
Every month (Rad_m)	**76%**	13%	7%	3%	7%
Once quarterly (Rad_q)	**81%**	11%	5%	3%	22%
Frequency of listening to music on other devices					
Every day (Med_d)	51%	**23%**	**19%**	**7%**	51%
Every week (Med_w)	68%	**15%**	**11%**	**6%**	68%
Every month (Med_m)	**77%**	12%	7%	4%	77%
Once quarterly (Med_q)	**79%**	11%	6%	4%	79%
Once yearly (Med_y)	**81%**	12%	5%	2%	81%
Less than once yearly or rarely (Med_r)	**84%**	10%	4%	2%	84%
Never (Med_n)	**84%**	8%	5%	3%	84%
Time spent listening to music (hours)					
0h (Time_w0)	**85%**	8%	4%	3%	33.5%
1-3h (Time_w1-3)	70%	**15%**	**10%**	**5%**	51.5%
4-6h (Time_w4-6)	65%	**16%**	**14%**	**6%**	9%
7+h (Time_w7+)	63%	**16%**	**15%**	**6%**	6%
Date of last purchase					
3 months ago (Pur_q)	44%	0%	**36%**	**20%**	22%
Last year (Pur_y)	74%	**24%**	2%	0%	8%
More than a year ago (Pur_2y)	**77%**	22%	1%	0%	15%
Never (Pur_n)	**86%**	13%	1%	0%	55%

Clusters	1	2	3	4	Sample
Date of last recording					
3 months ago *(REC_q)*	11%	**54%**	**34%**	1%	19%
Last year *(REC_y)*	**83%**	2%	4%	**10%**	4%
More than a year ago *(REC_2y)*	**89%**	3%	3%	**5%**	6%
Never *(REC_n)*	**89%**	3%	3%	**5%**	71%
Album acquisition channel (3 months ago)					
Store Yes *(CD_SY)*	**45%**	0%	**36%**	**19%**	19%
Fair/street market copy Yes *(CD_FairY)*	**41%**	0%	**37%**	**22%**	2%
Free download Yes *(CD_FdldY)*	8%	**57%**	**35%**	0%	10%
Copy from friends/family Yes *(CD_FriendY)*	13%	**51%**	**37%**	0%	4%
Track acquisition channel (3 months ago)					
Free download Yes *(TR_FdldY)*	6%	**61%**	**31%**	1%	9%
Copy from friends/family Yes *(TR_FriendY)*	9%	**54%**	**35%**	2%	2%

Overrepresented indicators in bold.

Variables (labels for graphed variables in italics).

Correspondence analysis statistics: absolute contribution of variables to inertia and relative contribution of axes to variables.

Table A4. Sociodemographic characteristics: correspondence analysis (per thousand units)

	mass	qlt	inr	k=1	cor	ctr	k=2	cor	ctr
Occupational status									
Self-employed *(Freelance)*	12	1000	3	8	4	0	125	996	45
Employed *(Empl)*	59	998	17	-109	634	12	83	364	94
Unemployed *(Unempl)*	9	875	1	-78	874	1	-1	0	0
Homemaker, retired, with disability *(Hrd)*	50	1000	110	371	961	113	-75	39	65
Students *(Student)*	13	999	167	-897	948	170	-208	51	129
Personal situation									
Single, living with parents *(SingleH)*	32	999	163	-574	985	172	-70	15	36
Single/divorced/widowed/separated, no dependent children *(SingleI)*	19	994	6	139	953	6	-29	40	4
Couple w/children <18 at home *(Couple0-18)*	48	999	7	29	86	1	96	913	103
Couple w/children ≥18 at home *(Couple18+)*	22	1000	30	293	992	31	-26	8	4
Couple w/children ≥18 not at home and other *(Couple++)*	21	1000	43	359	974	45	-58	26	17
Habitat (thousands)									
Provincial capital *(HPrCap)*	62	975	3	-58	974	3	-1	1	0
>100 *(H100+)*	12	924	1	22	65	0	81	860	18
50-100 *(H50-100)*	10	589	0	9	30	0	-38	559	3
10-50 *(H10-50)*	33	409	0	10	409	0	0	0	0
<10 *(H<10)*	27	995	5	109	971	5	-17	25	2

	mass	qlt	inr	k=1	cor	ctr	k=2	cor	ctr
Household size (persons >15 years)									
2 or fewer (Hh1-2)	48	1000	27	190	992	28	-17	8	3
3-4 (Hh3-4)	75	1000	10	-94	988	11	11	12	2
> 4 (Hh4+)	20	998	3	-101	998	3	1	0	0
Age									
< 25 (A<25)	21	1000	184	-751	967	191	-138	33	91
25-34 (A25-34)	24	994	36	-293	895	34	98	99	54
35-44 (A35-44)	27	985	5	3	1	0	110	985	74
45-54 (A45-54)	23	991	10	154	829	9	68	162	25
>54 (A54+)	48	1000	120	395	957	123	-84	43	79
Sex									
Female (Female)	75	989	6	72	926	6	-19	63	6
Male (Male)	68	989	7	-79	928	7	20	61	7
Education									
Upper secondary or below (Edu1)	121	998	5	46	793	4	-23	206	15
Third-level graduate (Edu2)	10	1000	11	-261	979	12	38	21	3
Third-level post-graduate (Edu3)	11	994	19	-245	564	11	214	430	122
Cluster 1	742	1000	227	141	997	242	-8	3	12
Cluster 2	126	1000	454	-476	961	468	-95	38	262
Cluster 3	87	997	266	-438	960	273	86	37	148
Cluster 4	46	990	54	-146	278	16	234	712	578

Ctr: absolute contributions of variables to inertia

Cor: relative contribution of axes to variables

Table A5. *Music consumption motivations: correspondence analysis statistics (per thousand units)*

	mass	qlt	inr	k=1	cor	ctr	k=2	cor	ctr
Reasons for buying copied albums from fairs /street markets (FM)									
Convenient, Yes (FMconvY)	4	982	16	-173	15	0	1370	966	288
Money savings, Yes (FMmoneyY)	10	989	30	-32	1	0	1179	989	451
Reasons for downloading free (DLD)									
Convenient Yes (DLDconvY)	50	999	133	-1095	996	143	-60	3	6
Fast and immediate Yes (DLDfastY)	31	1000	86	-1123	994	92	-86	6	8
Money savings, Yes (DLDmoneyY)	63	1000	170	-1099	991	181	-101	8	22
Only one track wanted Yes (DLDtracY)	12	998	35	-1148	998	37	-17	0	0
Reasons for preferring free copies (CP)									
Convenient Yes (CPconvY)	14	990	32	-1013	989	34	-25	1	0
Fast and immediate Yes (CPfastY)	6	1000	14	-1017	992	15	-93	8	2
Money savings Yes (CPmoneyY)	21	983	47	-998	983	50	6	0	0

	mass	qlt	inr	k=1	cor	ctr	k=2	cor	ctr
Reasons for NOT buying originals									
Copy from friends/family Yes *(CPfriendY)*	41	983	7	-270	978	7	20	5	1
Download Yes *(DldY)*	57	997	95	-868	994	102	-49	3	4
Expensive Yes *(ExpY)*	312	957	25	164	724	20	93	234	89
Latest release not available Yes *(RnaY)*	31	999	25	602	983	26	-77	16	6
Little interest in music Yes *(NintY)*	67	994	76	685	910	74	-208	84	96
No time Yes *(NtmY)*	39	1000	32	608	1000	34	-8	0	0
Prefer radio/TV Yes *(PrefTVY)*	141	997	118	603	956	121	-126	41	73
Other reasons Yes *(OtherY)*	101	999	59	515	995	64	34	4	4
Cluster 1	588	1000	344	515	993	368	-44	7	37
Cluster 2	228	998	404	-888	976	424	-134	22	135
Cluster 3	146	990	200	-762	928	200	196	62	185
Cluster 4	39	974	51	289	138	8	711	836	643

Table A6. *Behaviour patterns: correspondence analysis statistics (per thousand units)*

	mass	qlt	inr	k=1	cor	ctr	k=2	cor	ctr
Frequency of listening to radio-broadcast music									
Every day (R_d)	84	819	0	-15	183	0	-29	636	1
Every week (R_w)	26	996	1	-93	810	1	45	186	1
Every month (R_m)	11	997	1	-120	693	1	80	304	1
Once quarterly (R_q)	34	991	6	-216	843	7	91	148	3
Frequency of listening to music on other media									
Every day (M_d)	68	983	38	422	970	52	-48	13	2
Every week (M_w)	43	528	0	43	519	0	-6	10	0
Every month (M_m)	10	999	1	-131	866	1	51	133	0
Once quarterly (M_q)	4	997	0	-198	949	1	45	49	0
Once yearly (M_y)	1	985	0	-200	670	0	138	315	0
Less than once yearly (M_r)	10	973	3	-272	849	3	104	124	1
Never (M_n)	173	992	45	-288	973	62	40	19	3
Time spent listening to music (hours)									
0h (T_w0)	52	984	17	-320	943	23	66	40	2
1-3h (T_w1-3)	79	165	0	10	86	0	10	79	0
4-6h (T_w4-6)	14	999	1	132	882	1	-48	117	0
7+h (T_w7+)	9	1000	1	171	775	1	-92	225	1
Date of last purchase									
3 months ago (P_q)	34	1000	134	461	164	31	-1042	836	376
Last year (P_y)	13	962	8	-49	12	0	431	950	25
More than a year ago (P_2y)	24	977	12	-103	62	1	397	915	38
Never (P_n)	84	997	42	-297	535	32	276	462	65

	mass	qlt	inr	k=1	cor	ctr	k=2	cor	ctr
Date of last recording									
3 months ago (REC_q)	29	999	198	1442	933	265	383	66	44
Last year (REC_y)	6	887	4	-357	601	4	-246	286	4
More than a year ago (REC_2y)	9	999	5	-435	972	7	-73	27	0
Never (REC_n)	110	1000	66	-441	983	93	-58	17	4
Album acquisition channel (3 months ago)									
Store Yes (CD_SY)	29	999	113	461	167	27	-1027	832	314
Fair/market: copied CD Yes (CD_cFY)	3	999	13	511	175	3	-1107	824	36
Free download Yes (CD_FdY)	16	999	118	1519	920	155	444	79	31
Copy from friends/family Yes (CD_FrY)	7	989	43	1420	941	58	319	47	7
Track acquisition channel (3 months ago)									
Free download Yes (TR_Y)	14	997	110	1534	891	140	530	106	39
Copy from friends/family Yes (TR_F)	3	1000	22	1466	952	29	330	48	3
Cluster 1	706	1000	189	-296	991	269	28	95	706
Cluster 2	139	998	360	766	687	355	515	311	376
Cluster 3	105	996	325	903	798	372	-450	198	216
Cluster 4	49	981	125	148	26	5	-901	955	402

Chapter 7

Law and economics of culture markets. Perspectives on incentives, selection, production and marketing

Jordi López-Sintas

Universitat Autònoma de Barcelona, Spain.
jordi.lopez@uab.es

Doi: http://dx.doi.org/10.3926/oms.304

How to cite this chapter

López-Sintas, J. (2015). Law and economics of culture markets. Perspectives on incentives, selection, production and marketing. In López-Sintas, J. (Ed.). *The social construction of culture markets: Between incentives to creation and access to culture.* Barcelona, Spain: OmniaScience. pp. 209-230.

Abstract

This legal, economic and social analysis of the evolution of copyright regarding cultural expressions highlights the socially constructed nature of the culture markets. The move from local to socially constructed global markets — where cultural expressions can now be consumed beyond the limits imposed by temporal and geographical distance — was made possible by technological innovation (as a necessary but insufficient condition) and by the legal configuration of cultural expressions as goods that could be bought and sold. The construction of global markets raises the problem of how to collect the royalties due from private and public reproduction. Our economic analysis of incentives to creation and access to cultural expressions suggests that the economic rights of creators should be distinguished from the financial rights of producers.

Keywords

Law and economics of markets, music industry, social construction, copyright, Internet, business model.

1. Introduction

Incentives to creation are based on the recognized need to both acknowledge authorship and guarantee authors an income from their work for a certain period (Scotchmer, 2004). Copyright law consequently has moral and economic dimensions. Whereas moral rights have been recognized since time immemorial, economic rights only acquired significance once production commenced on an industrial scale, thereby making works available to more consumers. This development of a market in cultural expressions —previously funded through a system of patronage — made it imperative to regulate economic rights (see White & White, 1993).

Literary, scientific and artistic creations have traditionally been produced collectively. Since reproductions were not feasible, influences could only be exchanged through geographical displacement of the authors themselves, their pupils or apprentices and people who publicized their works by word of mouth. We can take as an example the well-documented case of music (Peterson, 1990, 1997). Before recording became possible, musicians and performers interpreted their own creations, or versions of the creations of others, in their own local market, whose scope was limited by the transport modes available (Peterson & DiMaggio, 1975). Exchanges beyond these geographical limits resulted in creations that were more collective than they were individual. Although the influence of creators on each other was widely accepted, creators were recognized as the authors of their own works, and moral and economic rights were safeguarded by the locality of markets. Since earnings came from live performances at the local level, creators generally had no need for producers, publishers or collecting societies.

Performances were frequently collective works in another way, as they required, inter alia, sheet music, librettos, musicians, a conductor and producers to finance rehearsals and final staging. Indeed, in the case of classical performances, the need to maintain a stable orchestra meant that musicians had a working relationship with producers, as described for opera (McConachie, 1988; DiMaggio, 1982; Storey, 2003) and the early days of radio

(Peterson, 1990). Each performance was a unique collective effort, an experience that could not be canned and sold in markets different to those where production took place. Registered sheet music was, however, a particular case. Composers of classical music scores and librettos generally employed representatives to safeguard their economic rights. In other words, a market existed for these creations with economic value. This sector sowed the seed for subsequent changes in the management of author right, most especially when composers of popular music began to insist on protection for their compositions.

In local markets there were virtually no intermediaries — and therefore no conflicts of interest — between the artist and the consumer. Artists promoted themselves or, perhaps, employed a manager in return for a percentage of revenues. The relationship between performers /creators and consumers changed radically as soon as performances or works could be converted into products that could be enjoyed far from their origins. The printing press was the protagonist of the first major transformation of the market for cultural expressions. The printing industry rendered obsolete the scribes who handcopied original manuscripts as, not only were printed reproductions much more literal, they were also done much more efficiently and more inexpensively, thereby facilitating market expansion. Something similar happened with art works: a reduction in canvas size reflected the interest of painters to expand their markets and so achieve independence from patrons (White & White, 1993).

The reproduction of literary works by means of printing brought the publisher as a new player onto the stage. The publisher performed the functions of promoter, selected the printer and also chose who, what and when to publish. The gallery owner played a similar role in developing art markets (White & White, 1993). A distance was created between creators and their publics, who now transcended local boundaries, although, thanks to distribution networks, consumers were also moved closer to producers and publishers.

Several important changes occurred when the publisher who financed and selected works appeared on the scene, cultural expressions became an object with rights and information could be collected about consumer preferences and behaviour.

Initially publishers were self-regulating and, organized as guilds, they limited competition, reined in the bargaining power of creators and imposed price controls. Guild self-regulation eventually became regulated by law, which had the effect of curbing guild restrictions on competition. In return, however, guilds benefited from legally established copyright terms regarding the economic rights of authors, initially set at 14 years in Britain (Statute of Anne of 1710). Publishers were logically more interested in recouping their investment than in providing incentives to creation and innovation and so acquired powers in terms of selecting works.

Because publishers managed the economic rights of authors regarding (re)production for the period determined by law, a conflict of interest arose that produced asymmetry between parties with different negotiating capacities. Publishers, then as now, are obviously interested in maximizing revenues from their backlist overall, while authors are interested in maximizing revenues for their own works. To avoid this conflict, publishers would need to maximize revenues for each author they manage. However, this cannot be, as publishers have fixed resources and opportunity costs, so their resources need to be invested in works they expect to generate more revenues — typically new editions rather than reeditions.

Works that have remained in the public domain (off the publisher's backlist) are consequently reissued more frequently (Burrows, 1994). And this happens even though, for publishers who publish a work for the first time, the incremental cost of reedition is less than the incremental cost of a first edition for other publishers of works already published. Some economic researchers have consequently concluded that publishers should not have economic rights assigned to them for more than two years (Burrows, 1994), leaving other publishers to negotiate a reprint with authors without having to first obtain permission from the first-time publisher. What this amounts to is a separation of the economic entitlement of publishers from the intellectual property rights of authors. This perspective is especially important for governments interested in fostering creativity and innovation and broadening access to culture.

Another publisher issue is that of selecting works. It was hardly surprising that, until US legislation finally protected the rights of foreign authors, US publishers preferred to publish the literary works of English authors, not because they were better, but because they were guaranteed sellers (Griswold, 1981). This is the rationale behind publisher fairs held around the world (e.g., LIBER in Spain), namely to capitalize on books that have been successful in other markets. Language, unlike music (as we shall see below), has resulted in differentiated national markets for books.

2. Creation as an Individual Undertaking: National and Transnational Markets

The market for cultural expressions is socially constructed, as illustrated by Peterson (1997) in his excellent analysis of the country music market. Markets are constructed, moreover, on the basis of process innovations (in the past, printing, gramophone recording, etc) that have the effect of expanding sales.

However, innovation was not a sufficient condition in itself for the expansion of markets. The transformation of local into national markets required a legal framework to protect intellectual property and also the development of instruments and means for protection, copyright registration and fee collection. Furthermore, to transform cultural expressions into tradeable goods it was necessary to transform collective works into individual works invested with private rights. On transfer to publishers and producers, these private rights of creators were subordinated to the interest of publishers.

How the music market evolved is very illustrative (Peterson & Berger, 1971, 1975; Pererson, 1982). Local markets could only first be transformed into regional markets and then into national markets once producers decided to only issue works for which performers held copyright. Two important consequences were that it was necessary to create companies to register the rights of authors and it was necessary to limit access to the market (as had been done in the past by guilds).

The American Society of Composers, Authors and Publishers (ASCAP), founded in 1914 in the USA, was instrumental in converting artistic creations into goods (Peterson, 1990). Although ASCAP's creation — and new copyright legislation — was driven by successful authors and composers of the day as a reaction to potential revenue losses from gramophone records, ASCAP ultimately came to play a major role in restricting competition in the music markets (Peterson, 1990). Since none of its members would cut a master recording unless the performer owned the rights to their interpretation, other performers were prevented from achieving musical success with copies or alternative versions.

Since ASCAP had the capacity to decide which creations could be recorded and so be converted into a tradeable good, it had the effect of limiting variety, as it typically excluded newer genres from the regional and then national markets. As had happened some centuries previously with publishers, the major labels, and also the legislation, tended to favour the interests of intermediaries in the music markets of the day.

The consequences of the restriction of competition were multiple (Peterson & Berger, 1971, 1975; Lopes, 1992). Innovation was discouraged and newer musical genres were unable to access the market. These new genres, in fact, had to await a new process innovation — radio — to prise loose the restriction on competition, which came about also as a consequence of ASCAP's defensive reaction to the new radio stations (Peterson, 1985, 1990) acquiring prominence as an alternative source of musical entertainment. ASCAP's response was to impose abusive conditions and this led to a conflict with the National Association of Radio Broadcasters (NARB). To digress briefly, history seems to be repeating itself in Spain with the collecting society for music rights. Revelations regarding SGAE (which had already been brought before the courts on numerous occasions) and irregularities associated with its dominant position culminated in 2011 with a police inspection at its headquarters and destitution of Teddy Bautista as president (Flores, 2014).

ASCAP's abuse of its position and conflict with the NARB inspired the creation of a new performing rights company, Broadcast Music Inc (BMI). Its immediate impact was to reduce the royalties to be paid by US radio stations. However, its most important impact was that it enabled new musical genres to finally enter the market and so meet the demand of a new set of consumers avid for novel musical rhythms.

Thus, while record labels focused on record sales and on live concerts in regional markets, radio eventually had the effect of transforming those regional markets into national markets — with innovation again paving the way. Up to this point, the major labels were favoured by the fact that support media for records were very fragile and distribution channels had high fixed costs. The advent of radio combined with the invention of vinyl records (33 rpm and 45 rpm) — and later the CD — changed the distribution mode and enabled new labels representing newer music genres to acquire a foothold in the market.

Another innovation was television, which would later drive similar changes in the film industry. Since new legislation reproduced the market structure of radio stations — a few channels but nationwide — television ultimately played a liberalizing role. Large radio stations moved into the television sector with their technical and artistic teams (presenters, orchestras, etc). The reasons for restrictions on radio stations evaporated and the market was opened up, with many of the new radio stations specializing in music of different genres.

Again it was the law which, given an innovation, helped build a new market reflecting the interests of the most influential business sectors. And again we see the important role played by legal monopolies. Rather than produce content, television channels and radio stations distribute intangible cultural expressions, although they may do both. Spanish legislation requires television channels to produce films by Spanish directors; hence, television has been one of the main producers of content, including series — although series have more recently tended to be produced by private companies (López-Sintas, García-Álvarez, & Rojas de Francisco, 2013).

From an economic point of view, restrictions on competition are only justified when fixed and sunk costs of production are high and revenues are uncertain, as happens with book publishing (Caves, 2000). Legislation to restrict competition in markets has an impact on fixed costs (Seaman, 1981); thus, when market entry was restricted for radio stations, many activities were internalized, resulting in high fixed costs (Caves, 2000). However, once the main radio stations moved into television, the market for licences opened up and fixed costs were reduced. This is yet more evidence of how cultural organizations are both socially and legally constructed.

Publishers, record labels, radio stations, television channels, art galleries, etc, coordinate — albeit spontaneously — at different levels in the selection of cultural expressions (López-Sintas et al., 2013). Local and regional radio stations and television channels, the most innovative galleries, the smaller labels, etc, focus on newer, more avant-garde cultural expressions (see Hirsch, 1972), whereas their national corollaries choose from cultural expressions already pre-selected in niche markets. This process is entirely efficient from an economic point of view.

Nowadays, however, the hegemonic power of the major record labels and film producers transcends borders. For this to be possible, it was again necessary to transform legislation, this time through free trade agreements (under the auspices of the World Intellectual Property Organization, WIPO). New European legislation, too, effectively protected international rather than national production (Drahos, 2004). The problem, however, was how to collect royalties when public reproduction crossed borders. Since transnational strategies have the effect of increasing the fixed costs of organization, production and marketing, they are accompanied by demands for longer copyright terms. This was the case with lobbying efforts in the USA led by Disney, which resulted in the Copyright Term Extension Act, aka as the Sonny Bono Act or, more derisively, as the Mickey Mouse Protection Act (Lessig, 2001).

However, just when publishers, record labels and movie studios had created their transnational markets, along came the dematerialization of cultural expressions. The publishing industry had a trial run with the market for photocopies, which — although not resulting in immaterial expressions — did make possible the private copying of a public (library book) or private (friend's book) good. The typical response, in such cases, has been to defend continuance of the traditional business model while pocketing the extra revenues from private copying. Imposing a levy on any equipment or support medium capable of making or containing copies of cultural expressions was one solution — essentially little different from how collecting societies operate (in Spain, for instance, CEDRO for the book industry and SGAE for the music industry). With photocopying, as one example, the rights of consumers to make private copies clashed with the interests of producers. Despite the fact that Spanish legislation recognized that private copying caused minimal damage to the author (producer), all photocopies, digital players, CDs, etc, were required to bear a levy.

Collecting societies in Spain have become controversial, despite acting on behalf of their members and with government authorization. If there is no real control (whether administrative or market-derived), once they acquire a particular dimension organizations tend to take on a life of their own, defending interests which do not necessarily reflect their statutory powers or the ruling legislation. In Spain, poor government control over bodies that have accumulated vast resources over the years has led to behaviour and acts that can be described, at best, as irregular (Flores, 2014). These societies are not effectively monitored by the government (see Chapter 4) and their monopolistic control of the market affects public reproduction but also cultural expressions with potential to be converted into tradeable goods. As Padrós notes (see chapter 3), monopolistic collecting societies need to be suitably monitored and controlled by the administration in terms of negotiations regarding fees, mandatory mediation in conflicts and annual performance.

In a competitive setup, however, government oversight would not be necessary other than to regulate the activities of the various associations. This setup would require, however, effective dispute resolution mechanisms and the freedom for authors to choose between different collecting societies.

It is economically efficient for public performance rights to be handled by collecting societies so as to reduce overall transaction costs (Towse, 2001). However, yielding rights to collecting societies gives rise to certain agency costs, given that managers may not share the interests of their individual members — as happens in corporations where capital is widely dispersed (Jensen & Meckling, 1976). However, it would also be necessary to define exactly what is meant by public reproduction. Private copies may not be used for public reproduction purposes, yet they may be levied, as happens with the digital levy collected by collecting societies in Spain (see Chapter 4). Thus, although radio stations pay the corresponding reproduction rights, consumers pay again when they record broadcasts for private use.

As demonstrated by several studies (Liebowitz, 2005; Rob & Waldfogel, 2006), copying works held by libraries or friends do not all represent lost sales to publishers, labels or artists. These consumers, predisposed to pay less than the retail selling price, will not purchase a good at any price they perceive as too high or beyond their means. The evidence shows — regarding Internet downloads of music, books or films — that if, in a particular country, average income is half and prices are double those of the country of origin of the cultural expression, then it is only to be expected that consumers in that country will have a fourfold predisposition to copy (see López-Sintas, Cebollada, Filimon & Gharhaman, 2014). In all markets there will inevitably be people who copy because they want a good but are not willing or able to pay the market price (Rob & Waldfogel, 2006). The same logic even applies to markets selling alegal copies (e.g., *top manta* in Spain); indeed, producers can even manage the actual size of these markets by setting prices at a sufficiently low level to increase sales while leaving room for private copying or the purchase of copies (Dolan & Simon 1996: Ch. 6).

3. Creation as a Collective Undertaking: Global Markets

Rights collecting societies are experiencing a boom from the immaterialization of cultural expressions. Immaterialization, much more than just a change in support, implies changes in the production, organization and marketing of cultural expressions, as reflected in changes in market size and in the fixed and incremental costs of producing an additional unit.

With globalization, transnational markets have become global markets. Immaterialization means that a good can be made available immediately to a consumer anywhere in the entire world. Commercial platforms such as Apple's iTunes, Amazon, etc, sell and despatch digital goods anywhere in the world in less than a minute. The major producers and publishers of cultural expressions have lost control and influence over what consumers hear, view or read and over consumer tastes in general.

These changes have had a destructive effect on the star system so characteristic of the film, music and literary sectors. Commercial streaming platforms like Spotify, the outcome of initiatives to share cultural expressions, have aggravated this trend. Spotify's streaming business, based on thousands or millions of interpretations, is, in fact, a distributor and collecting society rolled into one, but more efficient than traditional models — at least in terms of collecting and distributing fees, in regard to which they also compete with producers and collecting societies. Streaming is likely to negatively affect music sales, whether in physical (Amazon) or digital (iTunes) formats (Aguilar & Waldfogel, 2015) — just as radio affected gramophone sales almost a century earlier.

Another change has occurred in terms of information. Producers and publishers in transnational and national markets were able to collect detailed information on market behaviour through their large networks of independent distribution outlets, whereas the outlets themselves had only a partial (local) vision of the market. Full information nowadays is in the hands of enormous corporations like iTunes, Amazon and Spotify. Producers, like the distribution outlets of before, have only partial information: they can know the volume sold but not its geographical and social distribution.

Significant changes are also evident in relation to creation and innovation. Since many cultural expressions are available online and many creators allow non-commercial use of their work provided the source is cited (Creative Commons licensing; see Elkin-Koren, 2005), cultural expressions are frequently collective endeavours. One such example is R, a language and environment for statistical computing and graphics (R Development Core Team, 2015) licensed under a Creative Commons licence. Many data analysis books that explain R are based on other books published either under Creative Commons licences or according to a marketing model whereby users pay what they feel the book is worth to them.

The digitization of production has also transformed production and marketing costs in the publishing, music and audiovisual sectors by reducing the cost of producing the first unit. Obviously there will always be blockbusters with high fixed costs, but, overall, fixed costs have fallen compared with the situation in the past (Shaw, 2013). The case of distribution and marketing platforms is slightly different, given the high fixed costs of the infrastructure needed to meet peak demand; sunk coats, however, can be met by selling spare capacity in times of low demand (e.g., Amazon's AWS service). It is also becoming increasingly common for musicians and writers (via, for instance, Amazon) to finance the production of new creations, either directly or through crowdfunding platforms.

Yet another change has taken place in sources of revenues for creators. Whereas before music performers went on tour to promote their albums, nowadays the Internet is used to access consumers and promote live performances. Evidence regarding revenue sources is revealing (Connolly & Krueger, 2005): US record sales fell substantially in the twilight years of the 20th century and the early years of this century, yet attendance at live concerts increased, despite the higher cost of tickets. This transformation in revenue sources has had two effects. One has been the response of record labels, which now offer 360-degree deals (see Chapter 3). The second was the decline of the superstar system and the resulting decline in income asymmetries for different artists. In other words, the most famous performers in the transnational model were not necessarily the best, but heavy marketing meant they eclipsed others who may have been as good or better. Nowadays, however, record labels have little control over consumer tastes and so cannot maintain the superstar system. There are now far more artists with income streams but, since they are less differentiated in terms of popularity, income asymmetries have been reduced. This paradigm shift has been the best test possible of two alternative theories — by Rosen (1981) and Adler (1985) — explaining the stardom system and popularity.

The fall in fixed production costs not only suggests that copyright terms for cultural expressions should be reduced, but also that the circumstances for efficient allocation of resources have changed. We no longer achieve better allocation of resources by excluding consumers who are less willing to pay, even though this previously was the case, illustrated as follows: if the market size was $n+k$, where n represented the consumers willing to pay a sum p_n, and where k represented the consumers willing to pay a sum p_k, then, if $p_k<p_n$, assigning production to n rather than to k ensured efficient allocation. Nowadays, however, since incremental costs are close to zero, efficient allocation is determined by that price at which the sum of all incomes is equal to or greater than total incremental costs.

The response of traditional producers and publishers has been so reactionary that the new models for marketing digital cultural expressions have come from companies outside the music, publishing and audiovisual worlds, namely iTunes, Amazon and Netflix. We have witnessed this phenomenon before: the earliest innovations in discography came from manufacturers of gramophones and recording media (e.g., the United States Gramophone Company, which eventually became part of EMI). Although later transformations within the same model were led by the labels, the switch from material to immaterial supports was again led by digital technology companies outside the music sector with an innate ability to understand trends.

The strategies used by companies to deal with unauthorized sales are varied. Powerful US corporations and rights management monopolists lobby for legislative changes to protect their revenues and business model and thereafter make changes to their pricing strategies. Once markets are no longer naturally segmented (e.g., once free movement of goods was allowed within Europe), given interdependencies between segments, companies have to maximize revenues overall (see Dolan & Simon, 1996) and not just for each market separately. A variant on the market segmentation problem is the existence of unauthorized, or grey, markets. On acknowledging the existence of a grey market, we also acknowledge segmentation. Thus, price-sensitive consumers buy in the unauthorized market, whereas the remaining consumers buy in the authorized market. In such cases, companies can design a pricing strategy that determines the size of each segment and so maximize the respective contributions to profits. In the case of music, books and film, a reduction in the selling price will reduce revenues from existing customers but will increase revenues from new customers. The question is whether the loss in overall revenues from existing customers is offset by the increase in revenues attributable to new customers.

The evidence indicates that illegal downloading of books, music and movies represents minimal to no revenue losses (Liebowitz, 2005; Rob & Waldfogel, 2006). The question is whether downloading is interpreted as a problem of financial incapacity to pay or as an ethical issue whereby people download because they will not be punished (Moores, 2008; Rasch & Wenzel, 2013). In the first case, reduced prices and improved incomes are the solution (Aguilar & Waldfogel, 2015), whereas legislation is the solution in the second case. However, if the problem is genuinely the first one, punitive laws like Lassalle in Spain and Hadopi in France will have no significant impact on either the number of downloads or on company revenues.

4. Incentives for Creating, Selecting and Accessing Cultural Expressions

From the above it can be deduced that the cultural industries have several problems related to incentives to creativity, selection of ideas and of productions, marketing and financing.

The protection of intellectual property rights, at least theoretically, has been aimed at encouraging creativity However, those who finance ideas have to invest capital in producing a good that entails the risk of being a market failure. Not all music albums produce the same market return, nor do all ideas have the same fixed cost of development.

Independent selection mechanisms are at thus work in the market through independent producers — whether labels, publishers, galleries, etc (Hirsch, 1972; López-Sintas et al., 2013). These producers, who perform the initial selection of new ideas in local or circumscribed markets, can expect greater variability in income but have lower fixed costs. In contrast, the major producers operating in the global market have high organization, production and marketing fixed costs.

The central issue is the transfer and length of copyright terms. The evidence suggests that the rights of the creator should legislatively be separated from the rights of the producer. Economic analyses indicate that producers should have shorter periods of protection because they will always have a comparative advantage in terms of reeditions (Seaman, 1981). But because of the opportunity costs of production, many works are not reedited even when they have a market.

The marketing problem is a closely related issue. In the national and transnational model based on physical support (CD) sales, the marketing and selection problems were resolved by converting just a few performers into superstars through touring and heavy media exposure, including, most importantly, radio air play — often involving the bribing of disc jockeys (see Chapter 3; also Coase 1979; Hirsch 1972; Tschmuck, 2006). However, this approach was logically limited by the financial resources available. Although, according to Rosen (1981), hits corresponded to the best performers and composers, according to Adler (1985), they were fabricated on the basis of popularity built through radio air play. The new model of marketing digital cultural expressions reveals that the star-system business model was, in fact, grounded in popularity, with at best a nebulous link to quality.

Nowadays fixed costs associated with entering the market have been greatly reduced — and can even be funded by consumers (for instance, through crowdfunding platforms) — and promotion of music through the Internet is inexpensive or even free. Now it is the consumers and not the producers or disc jockeys who choose the hits (which might even mean that quality and popularity may be more closely linked; see Shrum, 1991). This fact rankles with producers, as they have lost control over a market that they configured to mirror their own interests.

As we have seen above, there has also been an impact on revenues. Nowadays, the CD is, for many interpreters, simply a promotion and marketing accessory, used to make them known and to build demand — so that they can go on tour, where the real money is to be made (Krueger, 2005). Before, the system worked in the opposite way: tours were the means of promotion and record sales were the main source of revenues. This paradigm shift explains the advent of the 360-degree deals by producers.

Among the different instruments available to encourage creation is public funding (Towse, 2001), which is efficient when creation implies a high risk. However, we are left with the problem of how to share economic rights between creator and financer. Public funding of films in particular also has a selection problem, whereas public funding of music faces a market access problem.

However, we can take a page from television, which functions as an audiovisual distribution channel funded by advertising or fees (López-Sintas et al., 2013). As intermediaries with different levels of quality and demand, according to whether they are local, regional or national, they can operate as selector mechanisms that screen works as follows: first through local channels, with lower average but more variable quality and serving smaller markets, next through regional channels, with less variability in quality and serving larger markets, and, finally through national channels offering higher and less variable quality and serving a very large market. Audience research would pinpoint the best works for broadcasting on regional and subsequently national television. Hence, the most innovative publicly funded works would ultimately gain access to the market, which would select and determine the economic value of works. This selection process is very similar to how record labels select new performers, whether groups or soloists, with collecting societies distributing fees among creators.

5. Conclusion

The market for cultural expressions (books, music, films, audiovisual productions, etc) is socially constructed, with process innovations (printing, radio, Internet, etc) and legislation together acting to transform unique cultural expressions into goods that can be reproduced and sold through technological platforms.

Innovations in this socially constructed market create problems of selection, financing, reproduction, distribution and marketing, all of which must be resolved in a balancing act between social wellbeing objectives and the interests of creators, producers, distributors and consumers. This reflects the need to balance incentives to creativity (restrictions on competition) with access to cultural expressions.

We have seen that it is desirable to distinguish between the intellectual property rights of creators and the economic rights of producers; specifically, copyright terms should be higher for creators and lower for producers. Terms should be fixed taking into account the fixed costs of creating the first unit so as to encourage the creation, production and reproduction of works, guarantee adequate revenues for creators and ensure broader access for consumers.

Selection for financing purposes and market access are other fundamental problems associated with cultural expressions, given that their value for each consumer cannot be determined until the good is consumed. Guaranteeing market access is as important as protecting intellectual property rights, since the latter are worthless without the former.

Markets are in constant motion, with each new technological innovation shifting the balance achieved after the previous innovation. These changes force new configurations of existing business models, which, by trial and error, are adapted to the new equilibrium — until the next innovation. Law and economics therefore need to cooperate closely in order to ensure that the socially constructed markets of culture maintain a balance between private and societal interests.

Acknowledgements

This research has been possible thanks to funding from the Centre d'Estudis i de Recerca d'Humanitats (CERHUM) at the Universitat Autònoma de Barcelona, the European Union ERDF Programme and the Spanish Ministry of Education and Science (Research Project ECO2011-29558-C02-01-E) and the Catalan Autonomous Government/Agència de Gestió d'Ajuts Universitaris i de Recerca (AGAUR) (Grant 2014-SGR-502).

References

Adler, M. (1985). Stardom and Talent. *The American Economic Review,* 75(1), 208-212.
http://www.jstor.org/stable/1812714

Aguilar, L., & Waldfogel, J. (2015) Streaming Reaches Flood Stage: Does Spotify Stimulate or Depress Music Sales? *Digital Economy* Working Paper 2015/05. Joint Research Center.
https://ec.europa.eu/jrc/sites/default/files/JRC96951.pdf

Burrows, P. (1994). Justice, Efficiency and Copyright in Cultural Goods. In Peacock A., & Rizzo I. (Eds.). Cultural Economics and Cultural Policies. Dordrecht/Boston/London: Kluwer *Academic Publishers.* 99-110.
http://dx.doi.org/10.1007/978-94-011-1140-9_8

Caves, R.E. (2000). *Creative Industries: Contracts between Art and Commerce.* Cambridge, Mass: Harvard University Press.

Coase, R.H. (1979). Payola in Radio and Television Broadcasting. *Journal of Law and Economics*, 22(2), 269-328.

http://dx.doi.org/10.1086/466944

Connolly, M., & Krueger, A.B. (2005). Rockonomics: *The Economics of Popular Music*. Working Paper 499. Princeton University. Industrial Relations Section.

http://people.stern.nyu.edu/wgreene/entertainmentandmedia/Rockonomics.pdf

DiMaggio, P. (1982). Cultural entrepreneurship in nineteenth-century Boston. Part II. Media, *Culture and Society*, 4, 33-50.

http://dx.doi.org/10.1177/016344378200400104

Dolan, R.J., & Simon, H. (1996). *Power Pricing*. New York: Free Press.

Drahos, P. (2004) The regulation of public goods. *Journal of International Economic Law*, 7(2), 321-339.

http://dx.doi.org/10.1093/jiel/7.2.321

Elkin-Koren, N. (2005). What Contracts Cannot Do: The Limits of Private Ordering in Facilitating a Creative Commons. *Fordham Law Review*, 74, 375.

http://heinonline.org/HOL/Page?handle=hein.journals/flr74&id=391&div=&collection

Flores, A.T. (2014). Los tres nuevos trucos de la SGAE para quedarse con derechos que no son suyos. 18 November. *El Confidencial*.

http://www.elconfidencial.com/cultura/2014-11-18/los-tres-nuevos-trucos-de-la-sgae-para-quedarse-con-derechos-que-no-son-suyos_472848/

Griswold, W. (1981). American character of the American novel: an expansion of reflection theory in the sociology of literature. *American Journal of Sociology*, 86(4), 740-765.

http://dx.doi.org/10.1086/227315

Hirsch, P.M. (1972). Processing Fads and Fashions: An Organization-Set Analysis of Cultural Industry Systems. *American Journal of Sociology*, 77(4), 639-659.

http://dx.doi.org/10.1086/225192

Jensen, M.C., & Meckling, W.H. (1976). Theory of the firm: Managerial behavior, agency costs and ownership structure. *Journal of Financial Economics*, 3(4), 305-360.

http://doi.org/10.1016/0304-405X(76)90026-X

Krueger, A.B. (2005). The Economics of Real Superstars: The Market for Rock Concerts in the Material World. *Journal of Labor Economics*, 23(1), 1-30.

http://doi.org/10.1086/425431

Lessig, L. (2001). Copyright's First Amendment. 48 UCLA Law Review, 1057.

Liebowitz, S.J. (2005). Economist's Topsy-Turvy view of Piracy. *Review of Economic Research on Copyright Issues*, 2(1), 5-17.

Lopes, P.D. (1992). Innovation and Diversity in the Popular Music Industry, 1969 to 1990. *American Sociological Review*, 57(1), 56-71.

http://doi.org/10.2307/2096144

López-Sintas, J., García-Álvarez, E., & Rojas de Francisco, L. (2013). La producción audiovisual iberoamericana y europea: la política cultural como puente para fomentar el desarrollo de la producción local en mercados abiertos. In Martínez Hermidia, M., Brandariz, J.Á., Lage, X., & Vázquez, M. (Eds.). *Comunicación y Desarrollo*. Buenos Aires, Argentina: La Crujía. 123-138.

http://dx.doi.org/10.1016/j.poetic.2014.09.003

López-Sintas, J., Cebollada, À., Filimon, N., & Gharhaman, A. (2014). Music Access Patterns: A Social Interpretation. *Poetics*, 46, 56-74.

http://doi.org/10.1016/j.poetic.2014.09.003

McConachie, B.A. (1988). New York Operagoing, 1825-50: Creating an Elite Social Ritual. *American Music*, 6(2), 181-192.

http://doi.org/10.2307/3051548

Moores, T. (2008). An Analysis of the Impact of Economic Wealth and National Culture on the Rise and Fall of Software Piracy Rates. *Journal of Business Ethics*, 81(1), 39-51.

http://doi.org/10.1007/s10551-007-9479-0

Peterson, R.A. (1982). Five constraints on the production of culture: law, technology, market, organizational structure and occupational careers. *Journal of Popular Culture*, 16(2), 143-153.

http://dx.doi.org/10.1111/j.0022-3840.1982.1451443.x

Peterson, R.A. (1985). Six constraints on the production of literary works. *Poetics*, 14, 45-67.

http://dx.doi.org/10.1016/0304-422X(85)90004-X

Peterson, R.A. (1990). Why 1955? Explaining the Advent of Rock Music. *Popular Music*, 9(1), 97-116.

http://dx.doi.org/10.1017/S0261143000003767

Peterson, R.A. (1997). *Creating Country Music: Fabricating Authenticity*. Chicago, IL: University of Chicago Press.

Peterson, R.A., & Berger, D. (1971). Entrepreneurship in organizations: evidence from the popular music industry. *Administrative Science*, 10(1), 97-107.

http://dx.doi.org/10.2307/2391293

Peterson, R.A., & Berger, D. (1975). Cycles in symbolic production: The case of popular music. *American Sociological Review*, 40, 158-173.

http://dx.doi.org/10.2307/2094343

Peterson, RA., & DiMaggio, P. (1975). From Region to Class, the Changing Locus of Country Music: A Test of the Massification Hypothesis. *Social Forces*, 53(3), 497-506.

http://doi.org/10.2307/2576592

R Development Core Team (2015). *R Project for Statistical Computing*.

https://www.r-project.org/

Rasch, A., & Wenzel, T. (2013). Piracy in a two-sided software market. *Journal of Economic Behavior and Organization*, 88, 78-89.
http://doi.org/10.1016/j.jebo.2013.01.009

Rob, R., & Waldfogel, J. (2006). Piracy on the High C's: Music Downloading, Sales Displacement and Social Welfare in a Sample of College Students. *Journal of Law and Economics*, XLIX(April), 29-62.
http://dx.doi.org/10.1086/430809

Rosen, S. (1981). The Economics of Superstars. *American Economic Review*, 71(5), 845-858.

Scotchmer, S. (2004). *Innovation and Incentives*. Cambridge: MIT Press.

Seaman, B.A. (1981). Economic theory and the positive economics of Arts financing. *American Economic Review*, 71(2), 335-340.

Shaw, Z. (2013) *As Music Production Costs Fall, Shouldn't Price Fall Too?* Mediapocalypse.
http://www.mediapocalypse.com/as-music-production-costs-fall-shouldnt-price-fall-too

Shrum, W. (1991). Critics and Publics: Cultural Mediation in Highbrow and Popular Performing Arts. *American Journal of Sociology*, 97(2), 347-375.
http://doi.org/10.1086/229782

Storey, J. (2003). The social life of opera. *European Journal of Cultural Studies*, 6(1), 5-35.
http://doi.org/10.1177/1367549403006001466

Towse, R. (2001). *Creativity, Incentive and Reward*. Cheltenham, UK: Edward Elgar.
http://dx.doi.org/10.4337/9781843767459

Tschmuck, P. (2006). *Creativity and Innovation in Music Industry*. Boston: Kluwer Academic Publishers.

White, H., & White, C.A. (1993). *Canvases and Careers: Institutional Change in the French Painting World*. Chicago, IL.: University of Chicago Press.

www.ingramcontent.com/pod-product-compliance
Lightning Source LLC
Chambersburg PA
CBHW082146230426
43672CB00015B/2852